MAY - - 2009

New Hampshire

NEW HAMPSHIRE BY ROAD

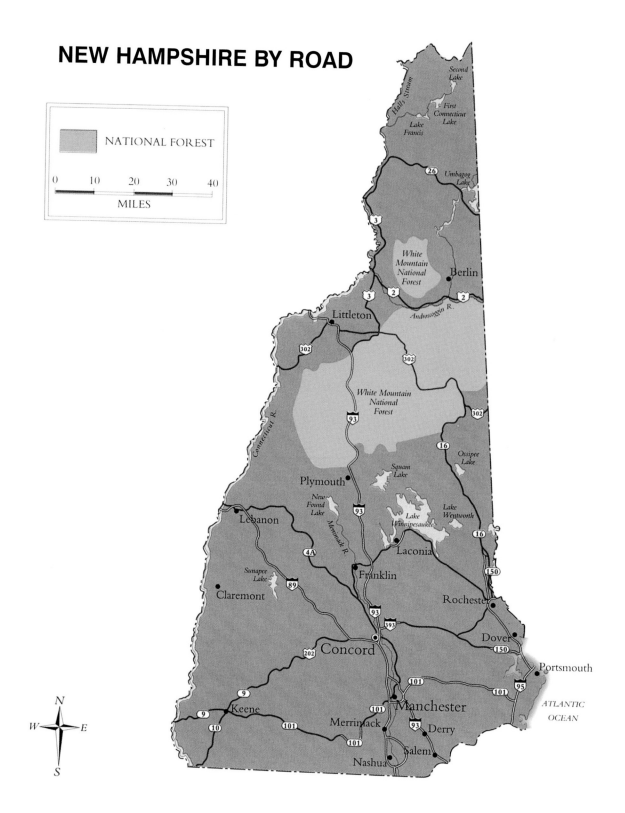

NATIONAL FOREST

0 10 20 30 40

MILES

Second Lake

First Connecticut Lake

Hall's Stream

Lake Francis

26 Umbagog Lake

3

White Mountain National Forest

Berlin

3 2

2

Androscoggin R.

Littleton

302

302

White Mountain National Forest

302

16

Ossipee Lake

Connecticut R.

93

Squam Lake

Plymouth

New Found Lake

Lake Winnipesaukee

Lake Wentworth

Merrimack R.

16

Lebanon

4A

Laconia

150

Sunapee Lake

89

Franklin

93

Rochester

Claremont

393

Dover

150

202

Concord

Portsmouth

9

101

101

95

9

Keene

101

Manchester

ATLANTIC OCEAN

10

101

Merrimack

93

Derry

101

Salem

Nashua

N
W E
S

Celebrate the States

New Hampshire

Steve Otfinoski

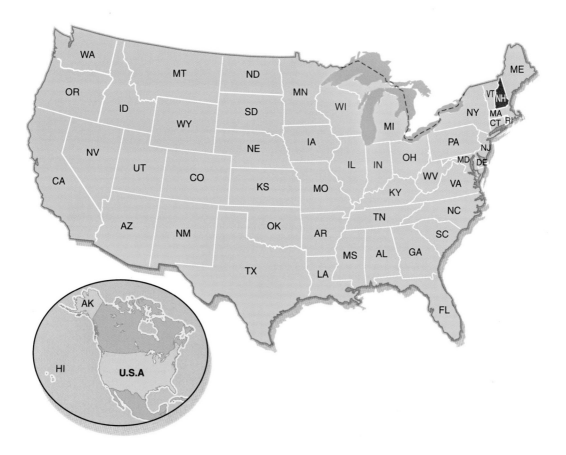

mc **Marshall Cavendish**
Benchmark
New York

Marshall Cavendish Benchmark
99 White Plains Road
Tarrytown, NY 10591-9001
www.marshallcavendish.us

All Internet addresses were correct and accurate at the time of printing.

Library of Congress Cataloging-in-Publication Data
Otfinoski, Steven.
New Hampshire / by Steve Otfinoski. — 2nd ed.
p. cm. — (Celebrate the states)
Summary: "Provides comprehensive information on the geography, history, wildlife, governmental
structure, economy, cultural diversity, peoples, religion, and landmarks of
New Hampshire"—Provided by publisher.
ISBN: 978-0-7614-2718-6
1. New Hampshire—Juvenile literature. I. Title.
F34.3O842008
974.2—dc22
2007009944

Editor: Christine Florie
Publisher: Michelle Bisson
Art Director: Anahid Hamparian
Series Designer: Adam Mietlowski

Photo research by Connie Gardner

Cover photo by David Forbert/SuperStock Photos

The photographs in this book are used by permission and through the courtesy of: *Getty Images:*
Altrendo Panoramic, back cover, 8; Dorling Kindersley, 10; Stone, 55; Harry How, 58; Hulton Archive,
130; *Corbis:* Bob Krist, 11, 99, 102; James Randklev, 17; Raymond Gehman, 22; Lewis Wicks Hine, 39;
Bettmann, 43, 64; Farrell Grehan, 53; Reuters, 59; Underwood and Underwood, 63; Dan Habib, 74;
Barbara Davidson, 80; FK Photo, 88; Jerry and Marcy Monkman, 92; Kevin Fleming, 95, 119; Dave G.
Houser, 96; Lee Snider, 105; Corbis, 125; Brooks Kraft, 127; Tim Zurowski, 109 (T); Jim Cosgrove,
128; *Alamy:* Jerry and Marcy Monkman, 57, 92, 134; Michael Dwyer, 12; Greg Ryan, 133, Brad
Mitchell, 137, NorthWind, 19; Philip Scalia, 48, 60, 82; Chad Ehlers, 101; *NorthWind Picture Archives:*
26, 28, 32, 34; *The Granger Collection:* 29, 35; *Art Resource:* National Portrait Gallery, Smithsonian
Institution, 37; *Kindra Clineff,* 44, 79; *Stock Food Collection:* Beery Photography, 61; *Gibson Stock
Photograph:* 97; *Frank Siteman:* 123; *Minden Pictures:* Sialia Sialis, 114; *AP Photo:* Tim Cole, 15,
70; Tim Boyd, 72; Toby Talbot, 76; Lee Mariner, 77; Joseph Mehling, 121; *SuperStock:* age footstock,
18, 51, 109 (B); *Dembinsky Photo Associates:* Marilyn and Maris Kazmers, 19; Jim Roetzel, 113;
The Image Works: Townsend P. Dickinson, 20; Image Works Archives, 30; Joe Sohm, 66; Julie
Henderson, 69; Mare Bernsaw, 106; Sean Cayton, 86, James Marshall, 84

Printed in Malaysia
1 3 5 6 4 2

Contents

New Hampshire Is . . .

New Hampshire is a beautiful state . . .

"Geographically we have a very unique state. One can drive from the White Mountains to the ocean in just a couple of hours. . . . People don't think of New Hampshire as a state for surfing, but it is one of the many activities available here."

—Michael Schuman, travel writer

"Hers [New Hampshire's], the majesty of mountain;
Hers, the grandeur of the lake;
Hers, the truth as from the hillside
Whence her crystal waters break."

—"Old New Hampshire," Dr. John F. Holmes

. . . with memorable landmarks . . .

"It seemed as if an enormous giant or titan had sculptured his own likeness on the precipice. There was the broad arch of the forehead, a hundred feet in height; the nose, with its long bridge; and the vast lips, which, if they could have spoken, would have rolled their thunder accents from one end of the valley to the other."

—newspaper account of the Old Man of the Mountain

. . . varied weather . . .

"I like how we get a bit of everything. We get a nice, warm summer, a cold, snowy winter, a mild spring, and a colorful fall with all the differently colored leaves."

—Allie Schuman, thirteen years old

. . . and an adventurous people . . .

"Motorcycling in New Hampshire is second to nowhere. There are a lot of beautiful two-lane blacktop roads that roll through the lakes and the forest."

—Clint Peterson of Ossipee

. . . who are fiercely independent.

"I'm proud to be a resident of a state that best exemplifies so many of the legendary characteristics of the mystical New Englander, even those not always considered by some to be attractive. I'm speaking of frugality, fierce independence, shrewd business sense, ingenuity—and not a little pride."

—Judson D. Hale Sr., editor in chief of *Yankee* magazine

"A rare sort of moral reckoning hangs over the most mundane acts here, as though each individual's freedom hinges on daily forgoing dessert and a second cup of coffee."

—Noel C. Paul, *The Christian Science Monitor*

New Hampshire attracts artists and writers . . .

"They [visitors] may go to Vermont for repose, but they come to New Hampshire for inspiration."

—Jim McIntosh, travel writer

"Nearly half of my poems must actually have been written in New Hampshire. . . . Four of my children were born in Derry, New Hampshire . . . . So you see it has been New Hampshire with me all the way. You will find my poems show it, I think."

—Robert Frost, 1938

. . . and, every four years, a host of politicians.

"We're so passionate about our primary. We believe we're one of the last places where, without spending a fortune, you can establish yourself as a viable candidate for president of the United States."

—Donna Sytek, former speaker of the New Hampshire House of Representatives

The old and the new come together in New Hampshire. It is one of the nation's oldest states. It is also one of the most modern, home to a thriving high-tech industry. It is a place of great natural beauty, inhabited by a proud and independent people. Come meet New Hampshire.

Chapter One

The Lay of the Land

The geography of New Hampshire is as fierce and unpredictable as its people. This rugged New England state boasts the highest mountain in the Northeast, Mount Washington, and one of the smallest but busiest coastlines. Even in the Granite State nothing is permanent. New Hampshire's long time emblem, a man's face carved by nature out of rock, recently crumbled from age and erosion. But the land reflects an independent spirit that has long attracted individualists, whether they be poets, artists, or high-tech entrepreneurs. For them, as for most residents, New Hampshire is more than a state. It is a state of mind.

MOUNTAINS, NOTCHES, LAKES, AND RIVERS

New Hampshire is one of the six New England states. Its neighbor to the west is Vermont. The two states fit snugly against one another like two pieces of a jigsaw puzzle. To the east lie Maine and the Atlantic Ocean; to the north, Canada; and to the south, Massachusetts.

The landscape of New Hampshire includes an Atlantic coastline to the east and interior hills and valleys.

Writer Dennis Fradin describes New Hampshire as "a slice of pie that wasn't cut straight." The state also resembles a key. It is broad at the bottom and narrow at the top, with one side flat and the other notched.

New Hampshire is the fifth-smallest state in total area, but its borders contain a great variety of landforms. In the southeast, New Hampshire has 18 miles of coastline on the Atlantic Ocean. It is the shortest ocean coastline of any state, but New Hampshire has made good use of it. The coast is studded with beaches that attract thousands of sun worshippers each summer. Hampton Beach, with its colorful amusement park, is the biggest. Six miles offshore are the Isles of Shoals, named for the shoals, or schools of fish, that swim nearby. New Hampshire owns four of the islands, and the remaining five belong to Maine. Fishermen and their families lived on these rocky isles for generations, but most are uninhabited now. Appledore Island is home to the Shoals Marine Laboratory, a laboratory and summer school operated by the University of New Hampshire and Cornell University.

Hampton Beach, located on the Atlantic coast, is New Hampshire's largest beach.

North of the coast, the New England Uplands cover roughly the southern half of the state. Through the uplands run the two most important rivers in New Hampshire—the Connecticut River, which divides the state from Vermont, and the Merrimack River. The Merrimack, which flows through the center of the state, provided energy for many industrial mills in the 1800s. The small cities of Concord, Manchester, and Nashua grew up along its banks. North of the Merrimack, before the mountains begin, lies a region of lakes. The biggest is Lake Winnipesaukee. There are more than a thousand lakes in New Hampshire.

Most of New Hampshire's northern half is dominated by the White Mountains, named for their bald, chalk-colored peaks. The greatest peaks are in the Presidential Range. Individual mountains are named for presidents Adams, Jefferson, Madison, and Monroe. All of these are more than a mile high. Towering above them all, at 6,288 feet, stands Mount Washington.

Lake Winnipesaukee, located in central New Hampshire, is the largest lake in the state at 71 square miles.

MOUNT WASHINGTON

"All my life I have admired and felt in awe of Mount Washington," says travel writer Skip Sheffield. Many New Hampshirites would agree with him. In addition to being the highest point in the Northeast, the mountain has a proud history. The Algonquin Indians considered Mount Washington a sacred place. In the 1700s early European settlers established hiking trails, some of which still exist. In 1869 a coal-fired, steam-powered cog railway was built to climb to Washington's summit. It is the oldest continuously run railway of its kind and has the second-steepest track grade in the world.

If you do not trust the train and do not feel like hiking, you can drive a car up the mountain. Do not try it from October to May, however, because the road is closed. During this time Mount Washington has some of the roughest weather anywhere on Earth, with wind speeds recorded as high as 231 miles per hour. The mountain gets an average of 15 feet of snow through the winter, and snow falls at the summit eight or nine months out of the year. The lowest temperature ever recorded in New Hampshire was taken atop Mount Washington on January 29, 1934: 47 degrees Fahrenheit below zero.

"I see more weather pass me in a week than most meteorologists see in a long time," boasts one staffer at the mountain's weather observatory. All in all, Mount Washington is one memorable place.

Far smaller, but just as fascinating, are New Hampshire's five monadnocks. These are age-old rocks so hard that they did not wear down as the rest of the surrounding land eroded over countless centuries. The most famous is Mount Monadnock in the southwest. It was a favorite hiking spot for the nineteenth-century authors Nathaniel Hawthorne, Herman Melville, and Ralph Waldo Emerson. Today, more than 125,000 visitors make the climb to the top of the 3,165-foot-high mountain each year. Few mountains on Earth have seen more climbers. "It's not so much a wilderness experience as it is a social happening," says ranger Ben Haubrich.

New Hampshire's most famous landmark was the Old Man of the Mountain, a face that nature carved into the rock. This amazing natural formation stood 40-feet high and looked over Franconia Notch, one of eight notches, or natural breaks, in the White Mountains. The famed rock formation collapsed on May 3, 2003. The Old Woman of the Notch still can be seen, however. She is less famous than her husband but has the added glamour of hair, formed by trees and brush.

THE DEVIL'S FOOTPRINT

Every natural formation in New Hampshire seems to have its own legend or piece of folklore. Take the Devil's Footprint, a formation near Milford. The story goes that the devil invited the men in the neighborhood to a dinner of baked beans. He cooked the beans in a big pothole amid the rocks, where he could trap the men after they ate. While he was dishing out dinner, the devil stepped on a rock made soft by the heat from his cooking. He could not get his foot free and started roaring in frustration. Frightened by the sound, the men fled and unwittingly saved their souls. The devil finally managed to get his foot out, but his footprint remains in the rock. Or so the legend goes.

LAND AND WATER

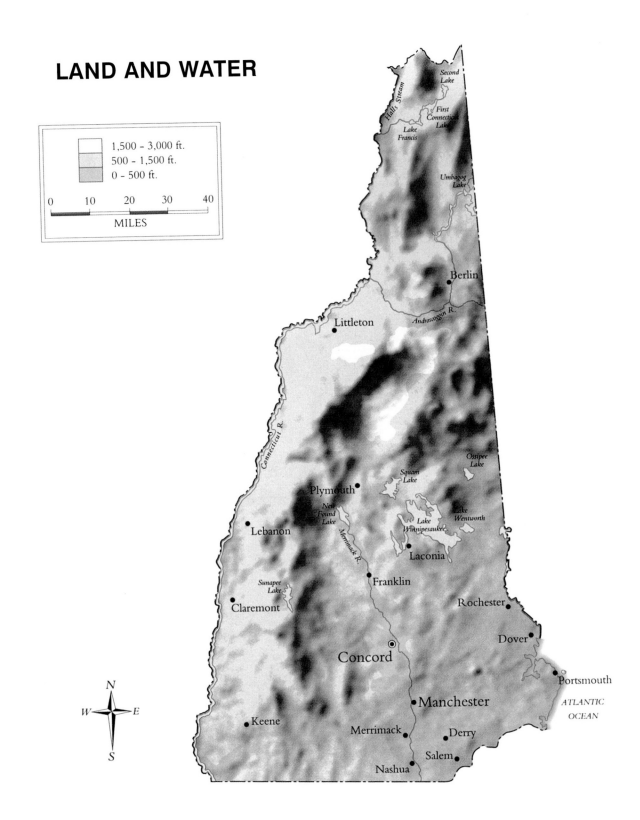

☐	1,500 – 3,000 ft.
☐	500 – 1,500 ft.
☐	0 – 500 ft.

0   10   20   30   40

MILES

N
W   E
S

Halls Stream

Second Lake

First Connecticut Lake

Lake Francis

Umbagog Lake

Berlin

Androscoggin R.

Littleton

Connecticut R.

Ossipee Lake

Squam Lake

Plymouth

New Found Lake

Lake Wentworth

Lebanon

Merrimack R.

Lake Winnipesaukee

Laconia

Franklin

Sunapee Lake

Rochester

Claremont

Dover

Concord

Portsmouth

Manchester

ATLANTIC OCEAN

Keene

Merrimack

Derry

Salem

Nashua

CLIMATE

New Hampshire is generally cool in the summer and very cool in the winter. This is a perfect climate for people who enjoy winter sports. The White Mountains receive an average of 100 inches of snow per season and are a magnet for skiers.

Spring is a brief but welcome relief after the long winter. Fall is brisk and chilly and filled with the beauty of autumn leaves and their brilliant colors. Thousands of southern New Englanders and New Yorkers make a yearly pilgrimage to see the foliage of New Hampshire. Each year brings the Fall Foliage Festival in the town of Warner and a pumpkin festival in Keene. Not all New Hampshirites are pleased by the influx of tourists, however.

During autumn New Hampshire's trees delight visitors.

"It's a spectacular time of year, there's no doubt about it," says one North Conway resident. "But the [Mount Washington] Valley absolutely comes to a standstill because of the crush of people trying to get through."

Worse than the tourists are the blinding blizzards that sometimes paralyze the state. Although blizzards are the most common natural disaster in New Hampshire, few are as well remembered as the hurricane that struck the state in September 1938. Most hurricanes that travel up the Atlantic coast never make it as far north as New Hampshire, but this one did. Thirteen people died in the hurricane. Half of the state's white pines were destroyed, and ten bridges were swept away. Winds at Mount Washington topped 180 miles per hour.

BIG TREES, WILD ANIMALS

Forests cover about four-fifths of New Hampshire. The only state with a greater percentage of forestland is New Hampshire's neighbor Maine. Ash, beech, elm, fir, maple, oak, and pine trees abound. The distinctive white birch is the state tree. Native Americans used every part of the white birch. They made its sap into sweet syrup and ground its bark into meal. They used the wood to make canoes and fashioned the bark into roofing for huts, as well as cooking utensils, baskets, and boxes. Today the hard birch wood is used for wood pulp, fuel, and material for spools and mop handles.

In the shadow of the big trees flourish such flowering shrubs as mountain laurel and rhododendron. Wildflowers, a joyful surprise to hikers, include black-eyed Susans, goldenrod, violets, and the state flower, purple lilacs. Early settlers carried the lilacs from England and planted them around their homes to remind them of their native land.

White birch thrive in New Hampshire's White Mountain National Forest.

Open fields come alive in spring as hundreds of wildflowers bloom.

Small animals thrive in New Hampshire's fields and forests. There are large populations of rabbits, foxes, raccoons, beavers, porcupines, and skunks. Amid autumn's fallen leaves, squirrels and chipmunks can be seen gathering nuts and seeds for the long New Hampshire winter. Game birds such as ducks and pheasants roam the woods and wetlands and make the state a hunter's paradise. Deer have made a comeback in New Hampshire over the past few decades. Black bears and moose, two of the largest land animals in North America, also prosper. There are so many moose in northern New Hampshire that Route 3 between Pittsburg and the Canadian border is known as Moose Alley. Drivers on this road often spot moose.

Moose sightings occur throughout New Hampshire.

RETURN OF THE TERNS

The tern, a beautiful seabird, was once a familiar sight along New Hampshire's narrow coastline. The Isles of Shoals were home to as many as two thousand pairs of common terns. By 1950, however, increased human development and a growing population of predators had driven the birds away. Birds of prey and other animals such as seagulls, foxes, and skunks had eaten many tern eggs and hatchlings.

In 1977 the New Hampshire Audubon Society began a program to bring back the terns. They drove away the gulls from Seavey Island in the Shoals. They planted tern decoys and played tern calls to entice the birds back. In a few weeks, six pairs of terns were sighted on the island. Today, Seavey Island is home to more than 2,500 common tern chicks and a growing number of other tern species.

The Audubon Society has kept two biologists stationed near Seavey Island, and workers continue to drive away the gulls. "Terns will not make it on their own," said Tom French, director of the Massachusetts Endangered Species and Natural Heritage Program. "Terns' success is directly related to the level of human efforts to protect them."

There are many more deer than moose, and they are a far greater annoyance to residents. As suburbs spread out into once-rural land, deer appear in many people's backyards and eat every plant in sight. In some places the situation has grown out of control. In 1970 the state banned deer hunting on Land Island, a 2-square-mile island in Lake Winnipesaukee. Twenty-five years later the deer population had nearly tripled. The deer had eaten almost every shred of greenery and were starving.

The state sent in a sharpshooter from Connecticut, who shot two-thirds of the herd. The deer meat, called venison, was distributed to homeless shelters throughout the state. Animal lovers and environmentalists condemned the killing, but the island's residents breathed a sigh of relief. Both sides continue to debate the thorny issue of how to prevent the deer from taking over again. Local hunters killed more than 11,000 deer in 2002 alone. Meanwhile, many residents are closing their land to hunters, whom they see as a greater danger than the deer.

The number of coyotes has also been steadily growing in New Hampshire. Today, an estimated six thousand live in the state. "I would wager there's not a town anywhere in New Hampshire that doesn't have resident coyotes," says wildlife biologist Kent Gustafson. "It's not unusual for anybody in the state to hear them yipping and yapping and howling." These wild creatures pose little threat to humans, but they attack and eat pets, especially cats. For this reason, coyotes are the only fur-bearing animals with a year-round open season for hunting and trapping.

POLLUTION PROBLEMS

New Hampshire has taken good care of its environment. In recent years the state has had the best record in the nation in reducing the poisonous gases and chemicals released by factories and power plants.

A research center in the White Mountain National Forest measures the amount of acid rain that falls in the region.

In March 2005, the state senate passed a strict bill to reduce emissions from state power plants, and air pollution has been cut 87 percent since 1987. The state's industries and utilities are among the cleanest-burning in the country.

This does not mean the state is pollution-free—far from it. The culprits are not in New Hampshire but in upwind states as far away as the Midwest. The pollution from these states' coal-burning utilities has an unpleasant habit of drifting over New Hampshire and other New England states. It has given the region the dubious title "the end of the tailpipe in the United States." This pollution contains dangerous chemicals that are brought to the ground by precipitation. This is called acid rain. Acid rain has polluted the state's waterways and killed fish and other marine life. It also has poisoned the root systems of trees in New Hampshire's forests.

A 2004 report of the Air Resources Division of the New Hampshire Department of Environmental Services reported that health-related costs to New Hampshire from this out-of-state pollution amount to more than $1 billion a year. The national Environmental Protection Agency (EPA) has often been lenient with power plants, which are the biggest polluters. Frustrated by this, New Hampshire joined seven other Northeastern states in a lawsuit against the EPA. New Hampshire and its neighbors are tired of living at the end of the tailpipe.

Chapter Two

A Proud Past

"Live Free or Die" is New Hampshire's state motto. Its people are so proud of the motto that they display it on their license plates for everyone to see. The motto is attributed to John Stark, the state's greatest general of the American Revolution, who added the words "death is not the worst of evils." Freedom has been important to New Hampshirites since the first settlers arrived in 1623. They craved freedom from attacks by Native Americans, from Great Britain, and eventually from the overbearing federal government.

Some people sacrificed their lives to defend New Hampshire's freedoms. Many others have found a reason to live in a state where independent thinking and action are highly valued.

THE FIRST INHABITANTS

In the beginning, there were the Native Americans. Native Americans probably arrived in present-day New Hampshire about 12,000 years ago, as the last huge glaciers began to retreat from the region. Native-American artifacts dating back some nine thousand years have been unearthed near Lake Winnipesaukee.

Men from New Hampshire volunteered their service during the Revolutionary War.

By the time Europeans arrived in the region, most of its Native Americans belonged to the Abenaki and Pennacook tribal families, part of the larger Algonquin nation of tribes. The Abenaki included the Pequawket and the Ossipee. In the summer they farmed corn, beans, and squash. In the winter they hunted deer, moose, and other animals. They lived in small villages of huts called wigwams. To make wigwams they formed oval domes by tying poles together. They then covered the domes with bark or animal skins. Although New Hampshire's Native Americans got along with each

The Algonquin built their villages using natural resources from the region.

other well, they learned to fight in order to defend themselves from their sworn enemy, the Iroquois, who lived in what is now upper New York State.

The first Europeans to come in contact with New Hampshire's Native Americans were fishermen fishing offshore for cod. They came ashore shortly before 1500 and traded with the Abenaki. The Abenaki traded beaver skins for fishermen's blankets, metal pots, and ax heads.

EARLY EXPLORATION

The first Europeans to explore what is now New Hampshire may have been Vikings from northern Europe. Some experts believe carvings on a boulder outside of Hampton were made by a Viking explorer in about 1100 C.E.

Italian explorer Giovanni da Verrazano may have gotten a glimpse of the White Mountains from his ship on the Atlantic in 1524. Frenchman Samuel de Champlain was one of the first Europeans to explore the region. He sailed into the mouth of the Piscataqua River in 1605.

It was the wily Englishman Captain John Smith who gave New Hampshire its greatest boost in European exploration. After his adventures in Virginia, where he helped found Jamestown—the first permanent English colony in North America—Smith sailed the seacoast of New England in 1614 and landed in the Isles of Shoals. He named them Smith's Isles after himself.

Smith returned to England and wrote a book about his travels, *Description of New England*, in which he praised New Hampshire: "Here should be no hard landlord to rack us with high rents. . . . [H]ere every man may be master and owner of his labor and land in a short time." Such promising prose tempted many Englishmen and women to risk the long ocean voyage and to begin a new life in New England.

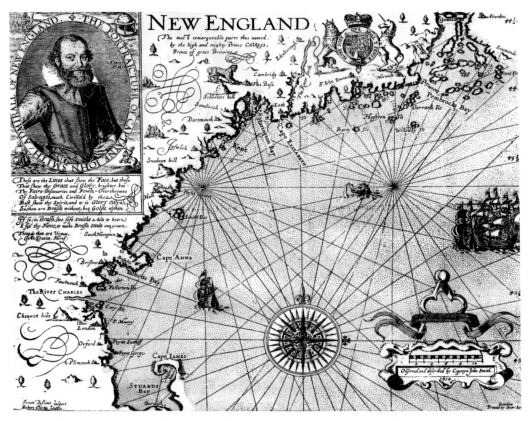

Around 1620 captain and explorer John Smith created this map of New England.

THE THIRD COLONY

New Hampshire became the third British colony to be settled, after Virginia and Plymouth. In 1622 King James I gave a large tract of land in New England to Sir Ferdinando Gorges and John Mason. In 1629 the two men divided their land. Mason's land was bounded by the Merrimack and Piscataqua rivers. He named it New Hampshire, after his native English county of Hampshire. Gorges's land, lying east of the Piscataqua River, later became Maine.

The four original settlements in New Hampshire are often referred to as the Four Towns—Dover, Portsmouth, Exeter, and Hampton. Dover, first called Hilton's Point, was established by Edward Hilton on the Piscataqua River in 1623. Colonists representing Mason settled on a hillside covered with wild strawberries in 1630. They called it Strawbery Banke. Colonists changed its name to Portsmouth in 1653. Exeter was founded on land sold to Reverend John Wheelwright by the Squamscott Indians in 1638. Colonists from Massachusetts founded Hampton the same year. A fifth settlement at Odiorne's Point was founded in 1623 but did not survive.

One of the four original settlements in New Hampshire was Dover, established in 1623.

By 1640 the Four Towns had about a thousand people—hardly enough, they felt, to sustain a colony. The following year they joined the Massachusetts Bay Colony for protection. Being New Hampshirites, however, they basically continued to govern themselves. They made their livelihood from lumbering in New Hampshire's rich forests, fishing its waters, farming the land, and trading furs. By the 1650s, a thriving shipbuilding industry had developed in Portsmouth, which had an excellent harbor. This rich heritage of shipbuilding is memorialized in the state seal, which depicts a frigate resting on the stocks in Portsmouth.

Settlers were attracted to Portsmouth for its economic promise in the fishing and lumber industries.

In 1679 the British king, Charles II, separated New Hampshire from Massachusetts and made it a royal colony. The two colonies were rejoined in 1689 and then separated again in 1692.

THE FRENCH AND INDIAN WARS

When the first European settlers arrived in New Hampshire in the 1620s, the Native Americans welcomed them. In 1644 Passaconaway, a great Pennacook chief, made a peace treaty with the settlers. The peace of Passaconaway lasted until the 1670s. Then colonial growth, slow but steady, came to be seen by the Native Americans as a threat. King Philip's War, a bloody war between British colonists and several Native-American tribes, broke out in New England in 1675. In New Hampshire, only the Nashua and Wachuset tribes joined the fight against the colonists. Other New Hampshire tribes sat out the war but formed an alliance with the French, who attempted to drive the British from North America in a series of wars known as the French and Indian Wars.

In 1689 a band of Pennacook warriors attacked the town of Dover in an act of revenge. Thirteen years earlier in Dover, several hundred Pennacooks had been captured through trickery and sold into slavery. The man who helped set the trap, trader Major Richard Waldron, was among those killed in the 1689 raid. In another raid, in 1697, Hannah Duston of Haverhill, Massachusetts, was captured by the Abenaki. While held on an island in the Merrimack River near present-day Boscawen, New Hampshire, Duston and the other captives killed ten of the twelve Abenaki holding them and escaped. The Abenaki eventually fled New Hampshire and moved to Canada, where they were later joined by the Pennacooks.

MAN OF PEACE

He was New Hampshire's first great Native-American leader. Passaconaway, whose name means "Child of the Bear," was chief of the Pennacook Confederacy, a group of Native-American bands living along the Merrimack River. About halfway through his long life, he saw the first English settlers arrive in his land. Passaconaway decided the only way to deal with these newcomers was to make peace with them. "I commune with the Great Spirit," he told his people in a famous speech before his death. "He whispers [to] me now—'Tell your people. Peace, Peace, is the only hope of your race.'"

When Passaconaway died in 1665, the legend goes, a pack of wolves pulled his body on a sled to the peak of Mount Washington. The sled, the wolves, and Passaconaway's body vanished in a cloud of fire.

THE AMERICAN REVOLUTION

The French and Indian Wars finally ended in 1763, when Britain drove the French out of North America. The colonists were unhappy when Britain imposed heavy taxes in order to pay its large war debts. Eventually their dissatisfaction led to revolution.

New Hampshire was the only one of the original thirteen colonies where no full-fledged battle of the American Revolution was fought. However, one of the first military actions of the war, before Lexington and Concord, took place in New Castle, New Hampshire. John Sullivan, a New Hampshire lawyer and politician, led a group of patriots in seizing military supplies from a British fort in 1774.

New Hampshirites made up for their lack of action on the home front by participating in the fighting elsewhere. New Hampshire volunteers outnumbered the combined soldiers from Massachusetts and Connecticut at the Battle of Bunker Hill. George Washington himself claimed New Hampshire soldiers were "far superior to the other colonies" in their "bravery and resolution."

Portsmouth, a center of New England shipbuilding, turned out three ships for the Continental navy, including the *Raleigh*, which was captained by naval hero John Paul Jones and is depicted on New Hampshire's state seal. About a hundred privateers operated out of Portsmouth. These vessels harassed British ships and stole their cargoes and supplies. New Hampshire general John Stark led American troops to one of their first and greatest victories over the British at the Battle of Bennington in Vermont in 1777.

Connecticut is known as the Constitution State because in 1639 it adopted the world's first written constitution, but New Hampshire could also lay a claim to that title. On January 5, 1776, New Hampshire

General John Stark leads his New Hampshire militiamen at the Battle of Bennington in Vermont, in 1777.

became the first colony to adopt its own temporary constitution and to create a government independent of Britain. The delegates to the Constitutional Convention of 1787 decided that the United States' Constitution would take effect when nine states ratified, or formally approved, it. On June 31, 1788, New Hampshire became the decisive ninth state to ratify the document. As part of the new United States, New Hampshire first established its capital in Portsmouth. (During the Revolution, Exeter had served as the capital.) In 1808 the capital was moved to Concord, where it has remained since.

Portsmouth was the state's capital until 1808.

A COUNTRY WITHIN A STATE

In 1832 New Hampshire was the scene of one of the strangest episodes in American history. The narrow northern tip of the state had been in dispute between the United States and Canada since 1783. Tired of paying taxes to both nations, the 314 residents of the 250-square-mile region declared themselves independent of both countries. They called themselves the Indian Stream Republic, after a stream running through the territory. For the next few years they remained an autonomous nation with their own constitution, legislative assembly, and forty-man militia. By 1836 the "republic" conceded it was part of New Hampshire, and the Webster-Ashburton Treaty of 1842 officially established the border between the United States and Canada. The center of the Indian Stream Republic was incorporated as Pittsburg in 1840.

WAR AND INDUSTRY

By the early nineteenth century, slavery was becoming a controversial issue dividing the South, which depended on slave labor, from the North, where slavery was less common. In 1835 Congressman John Dickson of Keene, New Hampshire, became the first person to speak out in the United States Congress against slavery. Daniel Webster, perhaps the greatest statesman to come out of New Hampshire, was more compromising on the issue of slavery.

New Hampshire had many stops along the Underground Railroad. This system of escape routes sheltered runaway slaves fleeing north from the Southern slave states toward Canada, where slavery was illegal.

Due to increased tension over slavery and other issues, the Southern states seceded, or separated, from the Union early in 1861.

GODLIKE DANIEL

In Stephen Vincent Benét's short story "The Devil and Daniel Webster," the great orator Daniel Webster wins a court case against the devil in a battle for the soul of a New Hampshire farmer. The real-life Webster (right) may never have beaten the devil, but his eloquence in the courtroom and on the floor of the U.S. Senate made him a legend in his own time.

Webster was born in Franklin (then part of Salisbury) in 1782. He became a lawyer at the age of twenty-three. He was elected to the U.S. House of Representatives, first from New Hampshire and then from Massachusetts, where he moved in 1816. He later became a senator and served as secretary of state to three presidents.

Webster was a man of boundless energy. It is said he rose every day between three and four o'clock in the morning, fed his cattle, and then worked until 9:00 A.M. "I have finished my day's work," he would say after breakfast, "written all my letters, and now I have nothing to do but enjoy myself."

Try as he might, however, Webster would never enjoy what he most wanted in life—the presidency. He ran unsuccessfully for the Whig Party's presidential nomination in 1836. Many Northerners refused to support him because of his willingness to compromise on slavery with the South. To Webster, however, nothing was more important than keeping the United States whole. In his most famous speech, in March 1850, he told the Senate, "I wish to speak today, not as a Massachusetts man, nor as a Northern man, but as an American. . . . I speak today for the preservation of the Union."

Less than a decade after Webster's death, his precious Union was shattered by the Civil War. It was a conflict he had done everything in his power to prevent. But this was one feat even the "godlike Daniel," as he was known, could not accomplish.

Within a few months, the Civil War began. An estimated 35,000 New Hampshire men answered the Union's call and fought in the Civil War. Nearly five thousand of them died.

After the North won the war, an industrial revolution swept through the East Coast. New machines could produce clothing and other products much faster than human hands could. Factories and mills sprang up across the Northeast. Immigrants, many of them from France and Canada, flocked to New Hampshire to work in the mills.

The largest, and one of the oldest, of New Hampshire's many textile factories was established in 1809 along the Merrimack River in Manchester. In 1837 the Amoskeag Manufacturing Company bought a 15,000-acre tract along a canal and built a self-sufficient industrial town where employees both worked and lived. By the early 1900s, Amoskeag was the largest textile manufacturer in the world. The company employed 17,000 men, women, and children.

Thomas Smith began working at Amoskeag as a child of fourteen in the early 1900s. He recalled working in the hot, dirty mills:

The hardest job I had in the mills was . . . cleaning out the picker machines. All the cotton seeds that came out of the cotton would drop down under the pickers, and we would have to go under there and get all those seeds. We'd have a wad of cotton in our mouth to filter out the dust and keep us from choking. It would be so hot, and we'd get that cotton seed on our skin, and it would hurt you something terrible.

Following World War I, Amoskeag fell on hard times due to stiff competition from newer mills in the South. By 1935 most of the company's mills were shut down for good.

Textile workers, including women and children, leave the Amoskeag Manufacturing Company after a day's work.

THE OLD GRANITE STATE

The Singing Hutchinson Family of New Hampshire wrote and performed antislavery songs from the 1840s through the Civil War. Below is their theme song, and they opened every concert with it. New Hampshire was called the Granite State because granite from local quarries was used to construct countless buildings in American towns and cities.

by Jesse Hutchinson

mu- sic, With a band of mu- sic we are pass - ing 'round the world.

We are all real Yankees,
We are all real Yankees,
We are all real Yankees,
From the Old Granite State.
And by prudent guessing
And by prudent guessing
And by prudent guessing
We shall whittle through the world. *Chorus*

Liberty is our motto,
Liberty is our motto,
Liberty is our motto,
In the Old Granite State.
We despise oppression,
We despise oppression,
We despise oppression,
And we cannot be enslaved. *Chorus*

Yes, we're friends of Emancipation,
And we'll sing the Proclamation
Till it echoes through our nation
From the Old Granite State.
That the tribe of Jesse,
That the tribe of Jesse,
Are the friends of equal rights. *Chorus*

DEPRESSION AND ANOTHER WAR

The 1930s were hard times for people throughout New Hampshire. A nationwide economic depression cost many people their jobs. Terrible floods in 1936 and a hurricane in 1938 cost some people their very lives. When the United States entered into World War II in 1941, thousands went back to work in the Portsmouth shipyards. They repaired warships and built submarines. Even the textile mills returned to life, as workers turned out uniforms for soldiers. Sixty thousand New Hampshirites served in the armed forces during the war.

POPULATION GROWTH: 1790–2000

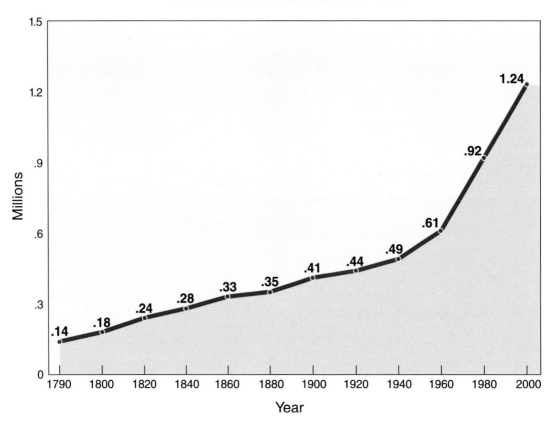

Even in the midst of war, however, New Hampshire was on the forefront of making peace. In July 1944, representatives of forty-four nations met at Bretton Woods in the White Mountains for a conference. This meeting led to the creation of the International Monetary Fund and the World Bank. These organizations were intended to promote free trade when the war ended and to help countries rebuild themselves through international loans.

The Bretton Woods Conference, a meeting of forty-four UN delegates, took place July 2, 1944, at the Mount Washington Hotel.

MODERN TIMES

The postwar years saw New Hampshire growing, as towns spread out and absorbed neighboring rural communities as suburbs. In 1963 the state came up with a novel way to raise money for public education. They instituted the first legal lottery in the United States since 1894. As other states followed New Hampshire's lead, lotteries became a common way for states to raise revenue.

In the 1970s the growth of the electronics industry brought new wealth and prosperity to southern New Hampshire. High-tech companies have found the region an attractive location both because it is near the big city of Boston, Massachusetts, and because it has neither a sales tax nor a state income tax.

New Hampshire today is a far cry from the agricultural state it once was, but the spirit of the state's founders is still very much alive. "Live Free or Die" is more than a motto on a license plate. It speaks for a people who value their independence above almost anything else.

Chapter Three

Natives and Newcomers

New Hampshire is a good place to live and to raise a family. In the whole state there are only some 1,300,000 people, about the same population as the city of San Diego, California. There are no crowded cities or sprawling urban centers, and New Hampshire has one of the lowest violent crime rates in the nation. "People here are a lot more down-to-earth than in other places," says writer Michael Schuman of Keene. "The lifestyle is relaxed. But where I live you're also only two or three hours from Boston and New York City."

These qualities, combined with the natural beauty of the countryside, have made New Hampshire an attractive place to live for many people. While most other states in the Northeast are losing population, New Hampshire has made some gains. The state added just over eight thousand new residents in 2005. "The kids raised here want to live here when they grow up," says former Nashua mayor Donald Davidson. "Great public schools, a revitalized economy, positive attitudes—we offer a better life for everybody. We're much more conscious of preserving what we have." In 2006 the United Health Foundation ranked New Hampshire the third healthiest state, after Minnesota and Vermont.

New Hampshirites take great pride in all their state has to offer.

ETHNIC NEW HAMPSHIRE

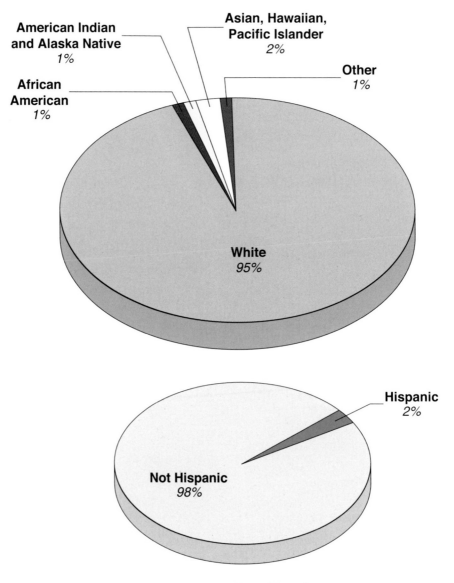

American Indian
and Alaska Native
1%

Asian, Hawaiian,
Pacific Islander
2%

African
American
1%

Other
1%

White
95%

Hispanic
2%

Not Hispanic
98%

*Note: A person of Cuban, Mexican, Puerto Rican, South or Central American,
or other Spanish culture or origin, regardless of race, is defined as Hispanic.*

GROWING DIVERSE

In the past, diversity has not been a hallmark of New Hampshire's population, but that is starting to change. Between 1990 and 2000, the Caucasian population increased only 10 percent, while the African-American population increased by 25 percent, Asian-American by 75 percent, and Latino (or Hispanic) by 81 percent. Still, minorities combined make up 5 percent of the total population.

LATINOS

There are about 20,000 to 25,000 Latinos in New Hampshire. Many of them have family roots in Mexico, Colombia, Puerto Rico, and Uruguay. There are also growing numbers coming to New Hampshire from the Central American countries of Guatemala, El Salvador, and Nicaragua, as well as Ecuador in South America.

The two cities with the largest Latino populations are Nashua and Manchester. Hector Velez, who moved to Manchester from Philadelphia, Pennsylvania, with his family more than a decade ago, became the first Latino elected to the state house of representatives, in 2004. "When I got elected, I started to see that what we don't see is what really moves and shakes the community," Velez says. "I started to see how legislation gets passed, how things that affect us at the state level really matter."

In September 2005 Governor John Lynch formed the Advisory Commission on Latino Affairs, an idea suggested by Velez. The commission's purpose is to advise the governor on legislation to improve the Latino community and to find ways to help Latinos enter the mainstream of society.

One important step in this process is encouraging Latinos to vote for political candidates who represent their needs. Getting out the Latino vote is the goal of Lillye Ramos Spooner, the first Latino woman to be appointed to the state's Commission on the Status of Women. "One of the things we do very well in New Hampshire is voter registration," she says. "We go from door to door, street to street, mobilizing people to get out and vote. Even though you're one voice, when many voices come together, we do make a difference."

ASIAN AMERICANS

The 2 percent of the state's population that is Asian American includes Southeast Asians, Filipinos, and Arabs from the Middle East. The state's most famous Arab American is U.S. senator John E. Sununu, who was

Asian Americans are a small but growing segment of New Hampshire's population.

raised in a large Lebanese-Palestinian family in Salem. His father, also named John, is a former state governor and White House chief of staff to President Ronald Reagan.

Many of New Hampshire's Asian Americans are Muslims, followers of the religion of Islam. Construction of the state's first mosque, a Muslim house of worship, began in Manchester in 2006. Zahid Malik, a member of the building committee, envisioned the mosque as not only a place of worship but also "a place where people get together, they share their problems. This place will not just be for Muslims . . . but will be open to people of all faiths." To prove this point, the Greater Manchester Interfaith Council has recruited volunteers from Christian and Jewish communities to help build the mosque. "There's no question that there is a tremendous heritage and history to Islam that the American people need to discover . . . which all the tragedies and terrorism have prevented many of us from seeing," says Chris Emerson of the Interfaith Council.

AFRICAN AMERICANS

African Americans make up 1 percent of New Hampshire's population, but their presence is strong. In June 2006 the University of New Hampshire in Durham held the first annual conference on the black experience in northern New England. The Dr. Martin Luther King Jr. Day Keep the Dream Alive Dinner has been held each year since 2000 under the sponsorship of the New Hampshire Cultural Diversity Awareness Council. This organization's mission is "to increase awareness of the need for communication, understanding and respect among people of ethnically and racially diverse backgrounds." It carries out its mission through educational programs, community events, and cooperative efforts with government agencies, schools, and corporations.

LEARNING ABOUT DIVERSITY

Each year a group of middle and high school students from around the state meet for a daylong conference on diversity sponsored by the New Hampshire Cultural Diversity Awareness Council. In February 2004, fourteen-year-old Cristina Vega, of Puerto Rican heritage, was one of forty students from Mastricola Middle School in Merrimack chosen to participate. She was pleased that her school system already promotes diversity. "We celebrated Asian, Hispanic, Indian, Jewish, and many other holidays," she says. "Being involved in those activities brought me to learn that other cultures and religions weren't wrong, just different from what I was used to."

The activities, talks, and discussions of the conference show students that understanding is something all of us have to work for. "Tolerance is an ongoing process," says thirteen-year-old Stephanie Greenland, another participant. "It's not always easy for people."

OTHER ETHNIC GROUPS

Native Americans make up 1 percent of New Hampshire's total population. While some Pennacooks remain in the state, all Abenaki now reside on two reservations in Quebec, Canada. Among whites, the state's largest ethnic group is French Canadian. Many French Canadians emigrated to New Hampshire in the nineteenth century to work in the mills and factories. They have kept much of their culture, their French language, and their religion, Roman Catholicism. Parts of northern New Hampshire have so many French Canadians that visitors may forget they are still in the United States. The other largest ethnic groups are Irish, English, German, and Italian.

Most of New Hampshire's population is a mix of people with heritages from Canada and Europe.

THE HIGHLAND GAMES

Did you ever toss a caber? Play a *clarsach*? Wear the tartan of your clan?

If you are a Scot, you know that a caber is a huge pole thrown in athletic contests, a clarsach is a Scottish harp, and a tartan is a woolen cloth woven with the design of your Highland family group, or clan. If you are not Scottish, you might still enjoy all these items at the New Hampshire Highland Games, held every September at Loon Mountain in Lincoln.

Each year 35,000 people attend this three-day festival of Scottish culture. Scotch-Irish immigrants were among the earliest European settlers in New Hampshire. The games give their descendants a chance to celebrate their rich traditions. Besides contests, feats of strength, and music (don't miss the bagpipe bands), there are representatives of sixty Scottish clans ready to help visitors learn about their heritage.

RELIGION

For many years, most New Hampshirites were Protestant. The church of the Puritans, called the Congregational Church, was the established church in each town. Until 1819 everyone was required to pay a tax to support the minister. Today more residents are Roman Catholic than Protestant.

Church attendance is not what it once was, however. Reverend Brad Bergfalk, the former pastor of a church in Concord, believes that the beauty of nature and year-round outdoor activities do not make for faithful churchgoers. "Nature becomes a substitute for traditional religious expression," he says.

There were very few Jewish people in New Hampshire until the early 1900s. The Shapiro House in Portsmouth's Strawbery Banke Museum was once the home of Russian Jew Abraham Shapiro and his family, who settled there in the early 1900s. Visitors to the museum can learn about the home life of one of New Hampshire's Jewish immigrant families. Sharon Kotok, a museum employee, says the exhibit "explodes the myth that all of these old New England locations were then populated only by descendants of the *Mayflower*."

A congregation attends Sunday service in Sandwich, New Hampshire.

POPULATION DENSITY

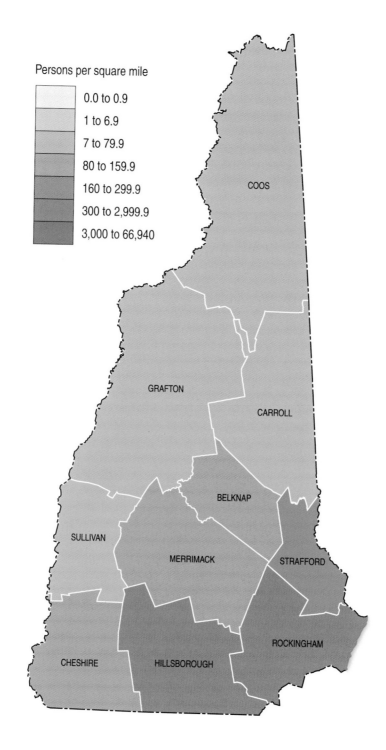

Persons per square mile

- 0.0 to 0.9
- 1 to 6.9
- 7 to 79.9
- 80 to 159.9
- 160 to 299.9
- 300 to 2,999.9
- 3,000 to 66,940

COOS

GRAFTON

CARROLL

BELKNAP

SULLIVAN

MERRIMACK

STRAFFORD

CHESHIRE

HILLSBOROUGH

ROCKINGHAM

THE OUTDOORS

When not working, the people of New Hampshire like to play. In the summer they enjoy hiking and mountain climbing. A group of adventurous hikers call themselves the 4000 Club. Each member has climbed all thirteen White Mountain peaks that top 4,000 feet. Hikers Dan Tetreault of Center Conway and one of his friends actually climbed all thirteen peaks in one day. They called it the Death March.

New Hampshirites take full advantage of outdoor recreational opportunities in their state.

"We ran into some other hikers up there," says Tetreault. "When we told them our plan, one guy said, 'You'll never make it in a day.' We snickered. Far from discouraging us, it put a spring in our step." By the end of the day, they were exhausted and barely able to keep going. When they finally made it to the top of Mount Webster, "I had a huge feeling of accomplishment and a big, goofy grin that didn't go away for days," Tetreault recalled. "It may have been called the Death March, but I've never felt so alive in my life."

Other people seek less challenging recreation during the summer. They enjoy swimming and sunbathing at the crowded beaches on the state's coastline or at the resorts along Lake Winnipesaukee.

Winter is for sledding, ice skating, and skiing, which was named New Hampshire's official sport in 1998. All these sports are part of the state's winter carnivals. One of the oldest and most popular winter carnivals is held at Dartmouth College in February. Snow sculpture is a favorite activity at the carnival. Groups of college students work tirelessly for days to create their colossal snow figures, some soaring as high as 30 feet.

Sports enthusiasts flock to the auto race held each July in Loudon. The race is three hundred laps long, a distance of just over 317 miles. It has never been won twice by the same driver.

Autumn is the time when thousands of "leaf peepers" from all over the country arrive in New Hampshire. "The colors of the leaves exploded and were aflame everywhere I looked," the late Jeff Smith, a chef who starred on television as the Frugal Gourmet, once wrote about a trip to Lancaster. "The white of the birch trees formed the canvas on which the colors were displayed and I was calmed. I swear I could smell the history of the colonies right in the air."

During the winter months, New Hampshirites enjoy cross-country skiing.

In July thousands pack the New Hampshire Speedway in Loudon.

HONORING THE PAST

New Hampshire's history can be smelled, seen, and tasted at its country fairs, a harvest tradition for generations. At fairs people enjoy such time-honored events as vegetable and livestock contests, games and rides on the midway, and dazzling nighttime firework displays.

Some New Hampshirites are so fascinated by their history that they bring it to life every chance they get. They stage reenactments of famous battles from colonial times. In July 1997 hundreds of history buffs gathered to reenact a siege by the French and their Native-American allies at Charlestown, once the northernmost British outpost on

HISTORIAN WITH A CAMERA

Among documentary filmmakers, few have brought American history to life more vividly than Ken Burns of Walpole. When his eleven-hour epic *The Civil War* aired in 1990, it became public television's most watched program up to that time.

Burns was born in Brooklyn, New York, on July 29, 1953. His father, an anthropology teacher and avid photographer, introduced both Ken and his brother, Ric, to the beauty of still photography at an early age. Still images later became a hallmark of both Ken's and Ric's work.

At Hampshire College in Amherst, Massachusetts, Ken Burns met his future wife and collaborator, Amy Stechler. She helped him with his senior-year project, a documentary about Massachusetts's Old Sturbridge Village, a re-creation of a typical New England town of the early 1800s. The couple moved to New Hampshire in 1979.

Burns's first professional film, which chronicled the building of the Brooklyn Bridge, ran only an hour but took four years of painstaking work to make. He also has made documentaries about the Statue of Liberty, baseball, jazz, and in 2007, World War II.

The Civil War was five and a half years in the making. Its use of still photographs and readings from letters and journals evoked the past in a fresh and exciting way. It set a new standard for historical documentaries and made Ken Burns a household name.

Why has this filmmaker looked toward American history for so many of his subjects? "My message has always been that history holds the key to the future," says Burns, "that is, by knowing where you have been, you can know where you're going."

the Connecticut River. The participants, who worked regular jobs on weekdays, were dressed as British soldiers, French marines, and Native-American warriors. If the French had won the siege, the course of history may have been very different. Northern New England and Canada may have remained in French hands for many years.

"These reenactors take their roles less as a weekend hobby than a constant sub-theme in their lives," writes journalist Keith Henderson. "Nearly every summer weekend is given to making history come alive."

Colonial reenactments in New Hampshire bring the state's history to life.

PUMPKIN MILK SHAKES

Pumpkin has been a favorite vegetable in New Hampshire since Native-American times. Most everyone has eaten pumpkin pie or roasted pumpkin seeds. But a pumpkin milk shake? Don't knock it till you've tried it.

2 cups vanilla ice cream
1/4 cup milk
1/2 teaspoon vanilla extract
4 tablespoons canned pumpkin
Dash nutmeg
Yellow and red food coloring

1. Mix the ice cream, milk, and vanilla extract in a blender.
2. Add the pumpkin and sprinkle in a dash of nutmeg for flavor.
3. Add a drop or two each of the food coloring to make your shake orange. Mix in.
4. Drink and enjoy!

AN ARTISTS' HAVEN

Creative people have always been drawn to New Hampshire, with its dramatic landscapes and live-and-let-live natives. Nathaniel Hawthorne was one of them. His story "The Great Stone Face," about the Old Man of the Mountain, made the rock formation one of the most celebrated natural landmarks in the country. Poets such as Joyce Kilmer; Robert Frost; and Donald Hall, the U.S. poet laureate, also have found inspiration in the New Hampshire landscape. Artist Maxfield Parrish was so taken with New Hampshire that he moved permanently to Plainfield. The mountain peak of Ascutney, which Parrish could see from the window of his studio, appears many times in his fanciful illustrations.

The artist who left the greatest mark in the state was perhaps composer and musician Edward MacDowell, who moved with his wife to a farm in Peterborough in 1896. After his death in 1908, his widow completed his plan for the MacDowell Colony, a haven for writers, composers, and artists. At this retreat, creative people can get away from the hustle and bustle of the outside world and devote themselves to their work. The grounds open to the public only one day a year, usually in August. On that day, the MacDowell Medal is presented to an outstanding artist, writer, composer, architect, or filmmaker. Among the famous Americans who have sought the solitude of the MacDowell Colony are writer Thornton Wilder and composer Aaron Copland.

Although they do not get invited to the MacDowell Colony, some of New Hampshire's most creative people have been inventors. Hair clippers, the machine lathe, and the hacksaw were all invented by New Hampshirites. Elias Howe hailed from Massachusetts, but he did some of his best work on his invention—the sewing machine—while staying in Nashua.

MAKER OF MONUMENTS

Each year about 2.5 million people visit the Lincoln Memorial in Washington, D.C. The man who sculpted the colossal statue inside it was Daniel Chester French, who hailed from Exeter.

French (1850–1931) worked for five and a half years on the famous statue of Abraham Lincoln. When it was finished and in place, however, he realized his work was not done. The bright glare off the memorial's marble floor made Lincoln's face look garish and grotesque. French decided that light shining from above was needed to make Lincoln look serious and dignified. It took him six years to perfect the lighting, but once he had, the statue at last looked "Lincolnesque."

In his lifetime French created many other famous sculptures, including *The Minute Man* in Concord, Massachusetts, which commemorates the Revolutionary War battle that took place there. His statue of George Washington on horseback stands proudly in Paris, France.

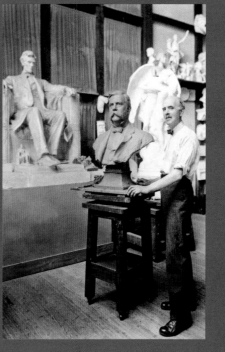

French's daughter, Margaret French Cresson, followed in his footsteps. She, too, became a well-respected sculptor.

Edward MacDowell is considered America's first internationally recognized composer.

Then there is Thaddeus Lowe, who was born in Coos County. He built a balloon in 1861 and flew it more than 500 miles, from Cincinnati, Ohio, to near Unionville, South Carolina. President Abraham Lincoln was so impressed with the possibility of using balloons for spying that he made Lowe chief aeronaut of the Union Army Balloon Corps. During the Civil War, Lowe successfully launched a fleet of observation balloons that provided a view behind Confederate army lines. After the war, Lowe continued to tinker. Eventually he invented the first ice-making machine.

Whatever brings people to New Hampshire—scenery, sports, or the freedom to create—many fall in love with the Granite State.

Chapter Four
The Democratic Way

Politically, New Hampshire is a study in contradictions. A refuge of bedrock Republicanism for decades, in 2006 it elected a Democratic majority to both legislative chambers of state government. Long considered the most conservative state in the Northeast, it has the only state constitution that acknowledges the right of revolution. New Hampshire's house of representatives has more members than that of any other state, but each legislator is paid only one hundred dollars a year. It has no state income tax and no general sales tax, but its property taxes are among the highest in the nation. On one thing, however, nearly all New Hampshirites will agree. They insist on having a say in how their government is run. New Hampshire has one of the most stubbornly democratic governments in the United States, if not the world.

INSIDE GOVERNMENT

New Hampshire's government, like every state's, is divided into three branches: executive, legislative, and judicial.

New Hampshire's capitol was built in 1819 and remains the oldest statehouse in the country in which the legislature meets in its original chambers.

Executive

The chief executive officer of New Hampshire is the governor. The governor appoints officials to state government, prepares the state budget, and recommends programs to the legislature. New Hampshire is the only state besides Vermont where the governor's term of office is only two years, not four. There is also no office of lieutenant governor in the state. Instead, New Hampshire has an executive council made up of five members. This council is a holdover from colonial times, when a royal council oversaw the governor's actions. Council members are elected to two-year terms. They advise the governor on important issues and approve all major appointments the governor makes.

From 1857 through the early 1960s, nearly all New Hampshire's governors were Republican. It was not always that way, however. Before 1850 the state voted staunchly Democratic. The Republic Party was started as an antislavery party, which gave it strong appeal in liberal New Hampshire. As the state grew in population, it became more conservative. So did the Republican Party.

Since the 1970s, New Hampshire has become more politically balanced as more Democrats have been elected to state offices. In 1997 Democrat Jeanne Shaheen became New Hampshire's first woman governor. "We are here to serve the people of New Hampshire," Governor Shaheen said in her inaugural address. "They are not interested in whether we are Republicans or Democrats, liberals or conservatives, men or women. What they expect from us is results, or at least an honest effort to achieve them."

Although she was more liberal than many of her predecessors, Governor Shaheen's emphasis on family concerns and education appealed to the people of New Hampshire. She served three two-year terms as governor and in April 2005 was named director of the Harvard University

Jeanne Shaheen was New Hampshire's first woman governor, taking office in 1997.

Institute of Politics in Cambridge, Massachusetts. New Hampshire's current governor is Democrat John Lynch.

Legislative

The New Hampshire legislature, which is called the General Court, has two houses—a twenty-four-member senate and a four hundred–member house of representatives. The only larger legislative body in the entire country is the U.S. House of Representatives itself. The legislature meets in the State House in Concord. Built in 1819, Representatives Hall remains the oldest chamber in the country in which lawmakers continue to meet in their original legislative chambers.

Governor John Lynch gives a state-of-the-state address in early 2006.

Because New Hampshire's legislators earn only two hundred dollars for a two-year term, they usually hold down full-time jobs in addition to their governmental duties. Along with making new laws, the state legislature passes the state budget and can propose amendments to the state constitution.

Judicial

The highest court in New Hampshire is the state supreme court, which has a chief justice and four associate justices. The supreme court evaluates whether laws or cases violate the constitution and whether cases from lower courts were handled correctly. New Hampshire also has a state superior court, probate courts, municipal courts, and district courts. All judges in the state are appointed by the governor and serve until they turn seventy, when they must retire.

In 1990 David Souter, a state supreme court justice, was appointed to the U.S. Supreme Court. Souter was born in Massachusetts and moved to a farm in Weare, New Hampshire, when he was eleven. Because of his long-time connections with conservative Republicans, many people expected Souter to uphold conservative positions. He surprised them, however, by becoming an open-minded moderate on the court.

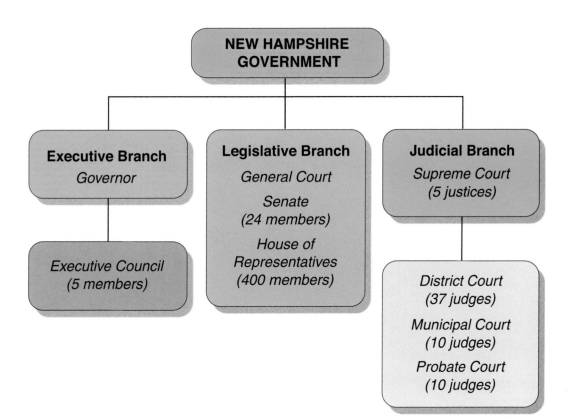

ON THE NATIONAL LEVEL

New Hampshire sends two senators and two congresspeople to Washington. In the 2006 election, the state elected its first congresswoman, Carol Shea-Porter. Shea-Porter's victory was all the more surprising because of her lack of political experience. A former social worker who volunteered with the Red Cross in the Gulf Coast after the devastation of Hurricane Katrina in 2005, she had never held political office. She had little money to spend on her campaign and relied largely on postcards sent to friends. Her stand against the war in Iraq and her support of workers' rights struck a chord with voters. She beat the Republican incumbent in a close race. Congresswoman Shea-Porter is determined to make a difference in Washington. "Instead of just sitting in the living room saying we should have ethics reform, I can actually do something about it," she has said.

Carol Shea-Porter (front row left) celebrates being elected as New Hampshire's first congresswoman.

NEW HAMPSHIRE BY COUNTY

COOS

GRAFTON

CARROLL

BELKNAP

SULLIVAN

MERRIMACK

STRAFFORD

ROCKINGHAM

CHESHIRE

HILLSBOROUGH

221 LITTLE REPUBLICS

State and federal government tell only half the story in New Hampshire. Self-government is so much a part of New Hampshire's communities that the state's 221 towns are often referred to as little republics. The voters in every town elect their own officials and approve how tax money is spent.

The foundation of self-government and the purest form of democracy in New Hampshire is the town meeting. Held once a year, the town meeting allows each citizen eighteen years of age or older to speak out on public issues. Then townspeople vote as a group to pass ordinances, to make town improvements, to elect local officials, and to deal with other business.

Citizens of Webster, New Hampshire, begin their town hall meeting with the Pledge of Allegiance.

"On town-meeting day . . . I would sit on the benches in the back of the town hall after school," Supreme Court justice David Souter recalls, "and that's where I began my lessons in practical government."

While New Hampshirites are proud of their freedoms, some question whether freedom should have its limits. They wonder where individual freedom ends and public responsibility begins. A good example is the state seat belt law. New Hampshire is the only state in the nation with no mandatory seat belt law for adults, although drivers and passengers under eighteen are required to wear a seat belt. Many residents attribute New Hampshire's high accident fatality rate to its lack of a stricter seat belt law. So far all attempts to pass an adult seat belt law have failed. However, a recent effort, backed by public-safety and health-care agencies, was the first to be endorsed by the New Hampshire State Association of Chiefs of Police.

"People might say they want to live free or die, but I always tell them live free and die, isn't that what you mean?" said state representative James Pilliod. He supports mandatory seat belts for adults.

Other residents see the issue differently. "It's another example of our Fourth Amendment rights being breached," said New Hampshire Libertarian Party chairman John Babiarz. "We believe people must be responsible for their actions. The responsible thing is to wear seat belts. But we feel this law is just another way of enforcing the nanny state upon us."

EDUCATION

New Hampshire has always been concerned about the education of its children. Some one-room schools from colonial times are still standing today, although few are still in use. The first public high school in the nation was founded in Portsmouth in 1830. The first free public library supported by tax dollars opened in Peterborough in 1833.

New Hampshire is also home to Dartmouth College, an elite Ivy League school and one of the ten oldest colleges in the country. Dartmouth was founded by the Reverend Eleazar Wheelock in 1768 as a department of his school for Native Americans in Connecticut. In 1770 Wheelock moved Dartmouth to Hanover, New Hampshire. Colonial governor John Wentworth wanted so badly to attend the first graduation that he had a 67-mile road built through the wilderness so he could get there. The governor might have been disappointed on his arrival—Dartmouth's first graduating class numbered only four men! Today Dartmouth is among the nation's best schools and has one of the largest college libraries in the nation.

As good as it is, the New Hampshire educational system has its problems. Since nearly all money for education is raised through property taxes, residents of poor school districts complain that their schools have less money to spend and are inferior to those in richer districts. Some schools are so underfunded that they have had to cut music and art classes—and some sports—just to have enough money to buy textbooks.

When Franklin High School senior John Costella played a basketball game at nearby Bow High, he was overwhelmed by how great the school looked. "They have computers in every class," he said. "I'm telling you, if I went to school there, every day I would kiss the floor."

Located in Hanover, New Hampshire, Dartmouth College is one of the oldest colleges in the country.

In December 1997 the state supreme court ruled that New Hampshire's system for funding education was unconstitutional. It said the state had to find a fairer way to fund all of its schools. The court gave state legislators a year to set new standards and to find a way to pay for them. The most obvious way to fund schools would be to create a state income tax, still a controversial topic in New Hampshire. Thomas Connair, a lawyer in Claremont, hailed the decision as "a courageous statement that the status quo in 'Live Free or Die' politics is unconstitutional."

Demonstrators protest New Hampshire's school-funding practices in front of the State House.

Another educational reform being considered is the statewide use of Real World Learning in high schools. This educational method, which allows students to earn high school credit through real-life experiences, including jobs outside of school, is already experiencing great success in isolated communities. The program seeks to keep more students engaged and in school. New Hampshire's high school dropout rate is about 20 percent.

"This is the first major education reform effort in New Hampshire since 1919," said state board of education chairman Fred Bramante in May 2004. "It's an enormous deal. It's absolutely revolutionary. We've known for years that kids learn in a variety of ways, so let's give them a variety of options."

THE KINDERGARTEN CONTROVERSY

Having no state or general sales taxes means that New Hampshire does not always have the money to fund programs common in other states. One issue that arises again and again is kindergarten. New Hampshire is the only state that currently does not have public kindergarten for all five-year-olds. This is upsetting for many residents, especially those who have moved to New Hampshire from other states.

The Sutcliffs moved to Hudson, New Hampshire, from Wyoming. Now they pay to send their five-year-old son to a private kindergarten. "We budget our house, our car," says Paige Sutcliff. "We didn't budget kindergarten." She and another mother have started a campaign to pressure state lawmakers to pay for public kindergarten statewide.

Some lawmakers have proposed to help communities start kindergartens with money from an increase in the cigarette tax. Many conservatives object, however. "We're opposed to the cigarette tax because we're opposed to tax increases, period," explains Roy Stewart, chairman of a group called the Granite State Taxpayers.

Because education is paid for primarily by property taxes, many New Hampshirites feel they are already paying enough for schooling. "Kindergarten is not the government's responsibility. It's parental responsibility," says state representative Bob Clegg. "The parents I've talked to in my community have said they want to keep their kids home. How do you tell them they need to pay for public kindergarten?"

Many educators argue that kindergarten is essential to the development of responsible students and citizens. "Kids at age five learn faster than kids at age six, and it slows down after that," claims state education consultant and early education expert Helen Schotanus.

Kindergarten is offered in only but a few of New Hampshire's school districts.

The struggle between New Hampshirites who want more social services and those who want to keep taxes low will undoubtedly continue. In 1997 Governor Shaheen approved a program promising state aid to communities that want kindergartens. However, the program did not specify where the money was going to come from. As of 2005, all but two dozen communities in New Hampshire provide public kindergarten.

A TAX HAVEN

New Hampshire is one of the few states that has no state income tax or general sales tax. It is no wonder that so many businesses, big and small, have flocked there. If there is one issue most New Hampshirites can agree on, it is no more taxes. In other states politicians promise not to raise taxes but often break the promise once they are elected.

THE PRIMARY STATE

Every four years, for about a month, the entire nation turns its attention to New Hampshire. The New Hampshire primary is the first—and many believe the most important—presidential primary. It was held for the first time in 1916. Since 1952 it has accurately picked the winner of the presidential election every time but once.

The New Hampshire primary has made national figures of presidential hopefuls such as Eugene McCarthy, George McGovern, and Gary Hart. In 1972 it ended the presidential aspirations of another candidate, Democrat Edmund Muskie, when he supposedly cried in public over accusations against his wife made by a local newspaper. When George H. W. Bush won the presidency in 1988 he closed his speech with the words "Thank you, New Hampshire."

The New Hampshire primary is so important that in 1997 a library and archives devoted to the primary's history opened in Concord. The library, the first of its kind in the nation, contains everything from books to campaign buttons. Although other state primaries are now clustered around the New Hampshire date, it remains the first primary. In the words of Terry Shumaker, a member of the primary library's board of trustees, the event is "a unique institution."

In New Hampshire, however, they are duty-bound to stick to their word. In the early 1970s archconservative William Loeb, publisher of the *Manchester Union Leader*, New Hampshire's biggest newspaper, came up with "the pledge." The pledge is a promise made by every person running for public office not to raise existing taxes or to support new ones, especially an income tax or a sales tax. Even liberal Democrats have taken the pledge.

Still, revenue must be raised somehow to pay for education and other public services. There are taxes on such products as alcohol, tobacco, and gasoline. Restaurant meals and hotel rooms are also taxed. Property taxes in New Hampshire doubled in just four years during the 1990s. This angered many homeowners.

A FAILING PARKS SYSTEM

New Hampshirites have felt the lack of tax revenue in the state parks and historic sites systems. Unlike other states that support both programs, New Hampshire funds them solely from user fees, which are not enough to meet expenses. Repairs and upkeep have been put off for years, and many cherished historic sites are falling into disrepair. The 120-year-old Robert Frost Farm in Derry is just one of numerous sites that is in desperate need of repair. At other sites, such as Daniel Webster's birthplace in Franklin, the parks system can no longer afford to conduct tours. "Parks being a self-funded agency, and to have the historic buildings included, is almost a formula for failure," said Allison McLean, director of the Frost Farm. Many residents support a proposal for the creation of a bureau of historic sites within the parks division, which is funded by tax revenues.

Chapter Five

A Changing Economy

In fifty years New Hampshire has grown from a state of small farms and midsize factories to become the nation's fourth most industrialized state. After a rough stretch in the early 1990s when it suffered an economic recession, New Hampshire's economy bounced back. It did so again, if less robustly, after the recession that ended in late 2001.

Economically, New Hampshire is in better shape than its neighbors, especially Massachusetts, which is still recovering from the recession. New Hampshire's unemployment rate remains consistently below the national average. Its resident labor force has grown by nearly 5 percent since 2001, and its gross state product in 2005 was over $55 billion.

NATURAL RESOURCES AND AGRICULTURE

Hard rock from the Granite State's quarries has been used in many famous structures, including the Library of Congress in Washington, D.C. The state has few other valuable minerals, however, so mining remains a minor industry in New Hampshire.

The lumber industry is an important sector of New Hampshire's economy.

A much more plentiful natural resource is timber. About 85 percent of the state is covered with forest, so the lumber industry is important. Cedar, pine, spruce, and other softwood trees are milled into paper and pulp. The once-flourishing pulp and paper industry, however, has suffered setbacks as the demand for paper products has shrunk in the digital age. In 2006 a major in-state paperboard mill and a pulp mill shut their doors. Lumber and other wood products made from hardwoods like ash, birch, and oak are still in demand, however. New Hampshire fir trees grace many a northeastern home during the holiday season.

One of the most popular products to come from trees is the rich, thick syrup derived from maple sap. The sap runs in late winter and is tapped through mid-April. New Hampshire produces about 69,000 gallons of maple syrup a year. Maple sugar and other maple products are gobbled up by natives and tourists alike.

Maple trees are tapped for their sap, a product that yields 69,000 gallons of syrup per year.

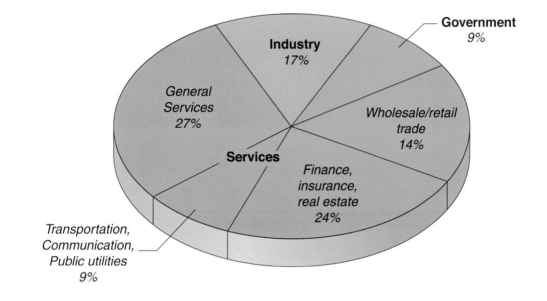

2005 GROSS STATE PRODUCT: $55 Billion

Government
9%

Industry
17%

General
Services
27%

Wholesale/retail
trade
14%

Services

Finance,
insurance,
real estate
24%

Transportation,
Communication,
Public utilities
9%

Today agriculture accounts for only about 1 percent of New Hampshire's gross state product. Fewer than two thousand farms remain. Many surviving farms are devoted to dairy products, especially milk and eggs—but even those are slowly disappearing. "When I was a kid there were thirty-five dairy farms [in the area]. Now there is one," said dairy farmer and retired speaker of New Hampshire's house of representatives Doug Scammon. "And you can't have all these farms here now." The reason for the decline is that land has become very expensive and is being bought up for housing and other development.

Remaining vegetable farms produce large quantities of sweet corn and potatoes. Fruits such as apples, blueberries, and strawberries grow well in New Hampshire's short growing season. Beef cattle and sheep are also raised in the state.

Agriculture is a very small part of the state's economy.

Fishing on New Hampshire's short coast has always been a thriving, if modest, business. Cod, haddock, and flounder are among the fish caught commercially in these waters. Shellfish such as shrimp and lobster also contribute to the fishing industry.

Inland, fish farming became popular as the number of fish in the oceans diminished in the 1990s. In ponds and tanks across the state, entrepreneurs raise fish such as flounder, salmon, and trout. Fish farming has its advantages. "Compared to cows and sheep, they never get out in the middle of the night and stand in the middle of the road," says Debbie Gile, a trout farmer, who previously tried raising livestock. "Nobody ever calls and says, 'Your fish are out.'"

NEW HAMPSHIRE WORKFORCE

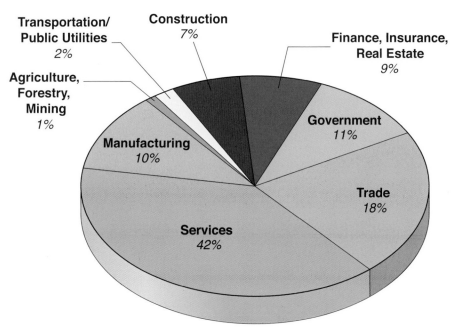

Transportation/ Public Utilities *2%*

Agriculture, Forestry, Mining *1%*

Construction *7%*

Finance, Insurance, Real Estate *9%*

Government *11%*

Manufacturing *10%*

Trade *18%*

Services *42%*

INDUSTRY AND TECHNOLOGY

The real backbone of the New Hampshire's economy has traditionally been industry. From early home industries to high-tech manufacturers, the state's factories turn out everything from machine tools and television equipment to farm machinery and shoes. The first shoe factory was established in Weare in 1823. Today New Hampshire is one of the nation's leading leather manufacturing states.

In the 1980s, however, the economy began to change. Many high-tech companies, especially those producing computer parts, moved into southern New Hampshire to take advantage of the state's low taxes. "The economy now in New Hampshire is no longer an old manufacturing-type economy," said Dr. Andrew King, director of the Survey Center at the University of New Hampshire. "It's service. It's high-tech, it's insurance.

Industry remains the largest economic sector in New Hampshire.

If you're going to come for those kinds of jobs, you have to have a college degree and often more."

New Hampshire's lovely countryside also attracts business. The city of Portsmouth, for example, has recently experienced a building bonanza, with two new hotels and the expansion of a third. Patrick Ford, president of National Hotel Realty Advisors, says, "[When] you come for business, and you get an opportunity to get around a little bit, you fall in love with the area."

NOUVELLE HAMPSHIRE

Many of the people who take these high-tech white-collar jobs are from other states, especially New York and Massachusetts. These newcomers are generally more affluent and better educated than the average New Hampshire resident. They had raised the per capita personal income to $37,835 by 2005, the sixth-highest in the nation. Today two-thirds of New Hampshire's residents are not native born. This has changed the character of the state. While there are still quiet towns and quaint country lanes, there are many new modern suburban areas. A writer for the *Washington Post* has called this modern-day state "Nouvelle Hampshire." The name has stuck, although some residents prefer to call their state "Massahampshire."

This "new New Hampshire" is inhabited by entrepreneurs who have moved there to open companies in the lovely countryside and to make money. They have been followed by real estate developers who have replaced the old downtowns with shopping centers and new housing developments. Even Manchester's old Amoskeag Mills have been converted into office space.

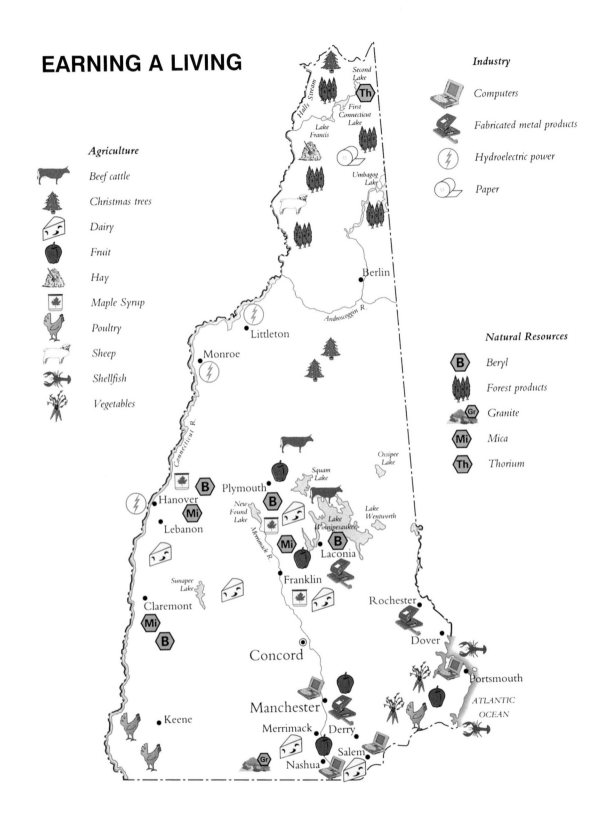

EARNING A LIVING

Agriculture

- Beef cattle
- Christmas trees
- Dairy
- Fruit
- Hay
- Maple Syrup
- Poultry
- Sheep
- Shellfish
- Vegetables

Industry

- Computers
- Fabricated metal products
- Hydroelectric power
- Paper

Natural Resources

- B Beryl
- Forest products
- Gr Granite
- Mi Mica
- Th Thorium

Second Lake
Halls Stream
First Connecticut Lake
Lake Francis
Umbagog Lake
Berlin
Androscoggin R.
Littleton
Monroe
Connecticut R.
Hanover
Lebanon
Plymouth
Squam Lake
New Found Lake
Ossipee Lake
Lake Wentworth
Lake Winnipesaukee
Mi
Laconia
Franklin
Sunapee Lake
Claremont
Merrimack R.
Rochester
Dover
Concord
Portsmouth
ATLANTIC OCEAN
Manchester
Keene
Merrimack
Derry
Salem
Gr
Nashua

Some people are concerned that this surge of new residents will bring new problems that New Hampshire has not had to confront before—crime, poverty, drugs, and other social ills common in states with large urban populations. Others are concerned about the progressive attitudes these new residents are bringing in, as they push for their local governments to provide everything from free snowplowing for senior citizens' driveways to curbside garbage pickup. Newcomers have even lobbied for laws requiring bicycle riders to wear helmets. "Everyone wants to wear a helmet now for everything," complains Jonah Couturier of Merrimack. "It's not government's job for that."

Still, even the most independent old Yankees see the benefits that newcomers have brought to their state, including an influx of money, prosperity, and more jobs, especially in the technical sector. Yet they miss the old ways. "The city is doing very well," admits Dick Avard, a small businessman in Nashua. "It's hard to put into words what we've lost. It's a way of life, no frills, a good and healthy lifestyle."

Whatever problems and qualms come with change, New Hampshire cannot look back. In the past, Yankee ingenuity has helped citizens to solve problems and adapt to changing times. There is no reason to expect otherwise in the future.

Chapter Six

A Grand Tour

The best way to get to know New Hampshire is to travel around it. Do visit the cities and larger towns, but also poke around in the state's more out-of-the-way places. There are a lot of nooks and crannies in New Hampshire, and each one contains a surprise.

SOUTHERN NEW HAMPSHIRE

Right across the Massachusetts border in North Salem lies one of the state's best-kept secrets—a 30-acre site of mysterious stone walls and large blocks of stone called monoliths. The site has been named America's Stonehenge because it closely resembles the huge ancient circle of stones in southern England. This Stonehenge is ancient, too. Archaeologists date charcoal found there to around 2000 B.C.E. Who erected these strange formations of stone? Adventurous monks from Ireland? Native Americans? Aliens? No one knows, but the mystery attracts 20,000 visitors a year to the site, which is owned, appropriately, by the Stone family.

A little farther west in Rindge lies another famous landmark. The Cathedral of the Pines is a church with no roof in a pine forest that faces

A backpacker enjoying the inspiring view of the White Mountains.

Mount Monadnock. In 1957 the U.S. Congress designated it a national memorial to the men and women who had been killed in war.

To the northwest is Keene, home of Keene State College, where many students train to be teachers. Keene's Horatio Colony House Museum is one of the state's most unusual museums. The fine old house, built in 1806, today belongs to Horatio Colony, a grandson of Keene's first mayor. In the museum Colony's family heirlooms are displayed alongside exotic souvenirs from his far-flung travels, including several bronze Buddhas.

Heading east again, we come to Nashua, New Hampshire's second-largest town. With more than twenty parks and the fine Nashua Center for the Arts, it has earned a reputation as one of the best places to live in the United States. Slightly north is Derry, where poet Robert Frost lived for over a decade. His homestead, the Robert Frost Farm, is a popular tourist stop. It includes displays on the writer's life and works, as well as a half-mile poetry nature trail.

A little farther north is Manchester. This is New Hampshire's largest city, although it is small by the standard of most eastern states. Once famed for its gigantic textile mills, today Manchester is known as much for culture as for industry. The Currier Gallery of Art, the state's largest museum, is famous for its collection of decorative art from New England, including silver, pewter, and early New Hampshire-made furniture. It also has one of the largest collections of glass paperweights in the world. Another Manchester site is the childhood home of the longest-living general of the American Revolution, John Stark, who died at age ninety-three and is buried in Stark Park.

A short drive north of Manchester is Concord, the state's tiny capital. Visitors who arrive during a legislative session can watch government at work in the State House. Those with a nose for history can visit Franklin Pierce's house, the Pierce Manse, which is now a museum containing the

Concord is New Hampshire's state capital.

fourteenth president's furnishings and personal memorabilia. Concord residents are proud of its being the home of a U.S. president, but are even more proud of New Hampshire's decisive role in ratifying the U.S. Constitution in 1788. A tablet marks the "birthplace of the United States" at the corner of Walker and Boutin streets.

Concord is also home to the Christa McAuliffe Planetarium, named in honor of the first civilian to go into space. Christa McAuliffe taught at Concord High School. She was one of 11,000 teachers who applied to become a crew member of the next space shuttle. McAuliffe won, and she trained hard for her flight on the space shuttle *Challenger*. It was to be the tenth trip into space for the *Challenger*, but bad weather and cold temperatures delayed the takeoff several times. On the frigid morning of January 28, 1986, officials gave the go-ahead despite objections from spacecraft engineers. Just seventy-three seconds into flight, the *Challenger* exploded and broke apart before the horrified eyes of the world. From an altitude of 46,000 feet the cabin fell into the Atlantic Ocean. All seven crew members were killed.

A little northeast of Concord is Canterbury Shaker Village. The Shakers are a communal religious sect that came from England just before the American Revolution. They got their name from the vigorous dancing that was an important part of their worship service. The Shakers were hard workers and built nineteen communities in the United States. Canterbury was founded in 1792, and by the 1850s it was home to three hundred Shakers.

At the Canterbury Shaker Village, visitors can see demonstrations of tools, furniture, and textiles being made.

The last member died there in 1992. Today the village is a living museum where visitors can tour the buildings that house Shaker-made textiles, furniture, and tools, renowned for their simple grace and beauty.

Portsmouth, another historic town, lies to the east, at the mouth of a river not far from the coastline. The state's second-oldest community, Portsmouth is best known for its naval shipyard, which was established in 1800. Modern submarines are now docked where frigates once were built. Revolutionary naval war hero John Paul Jones lived here while his warship was being built. The house where he lived is a popular tourist attraction.

Another impressive site is Strawbery Banke Museum, a restoration of the old Portsmouth seaport neighborhood known as Puddle Dock. What makes this 10-acre museum unique is the breadth of history it covers. Visitors can stroll through Portsmouth's past from the seventeenth-century Sherburne House to Abbott's Little Corner Store, which re-creates American life during World War II. Strawbery Banke really comes alive at the end of the year, with an annual holiday crafts fair in November and candlelight Christmas strolls in December.

The seaport neighborhood of Strawbery Banke cannot be missed on a tour of New Hampshire.

A POET IN NEW HAMPSHIRE

Many poets have found inspiration in the dramatic landscape of New Hampshire, perhaps none more than John Greenleaf Whittier. Whittier was born in Haverhill, Massachusetts, in 1807, and was a frequent visitor to New Hampshire. The following is part of a poem that depicts New Hampshire's most famous beach.

Hampton Beach

The sunlight flitters keen and bright,
Where, miles away,
Lies stretching to my dazzled sight
A luminous belt, a misty light.
Beyond the dark pine bluffs and wastes of sandy gray.

The tremulous shadow of the Sea!
Against its ground
Of silvery light, rock, hill, and tree,
Still as a picture, clear and free,
With varying outline mark the coast for miles around.

On—on— we tread with loose-flung rein
Our seaward way,
Through dark-green fields and blossoming grain,
Where the wild brier-rose skirts the land,
And bends above our heads the flowering locust spray.

Ha! Like a kind hand on my brow
Comes this fresh breeze,
Cooling its dull and feverish glow,
While through my being seems to flow
The breath of a new life, —the healing of the seas!

CENTRAL NEW HAMPSHIRE

Central New Hampshire is dominated by Lake Winnipesaukee, the state's largest lake. Covering 72 square miles and reaching a maximum depth of 212 feet, Winnipesaukee is the third-largest lake in New England and contains 253 islands. In the Algonquian language *Winnipesaukee* means "the smile of the Great Spirit." Anyone who has enjoyed its waters will certainly agree about the smile.

Small boats navigate in and out of the harbor at Weirs Beach on Lake Winnipesaukee.

PLACES TO SEE

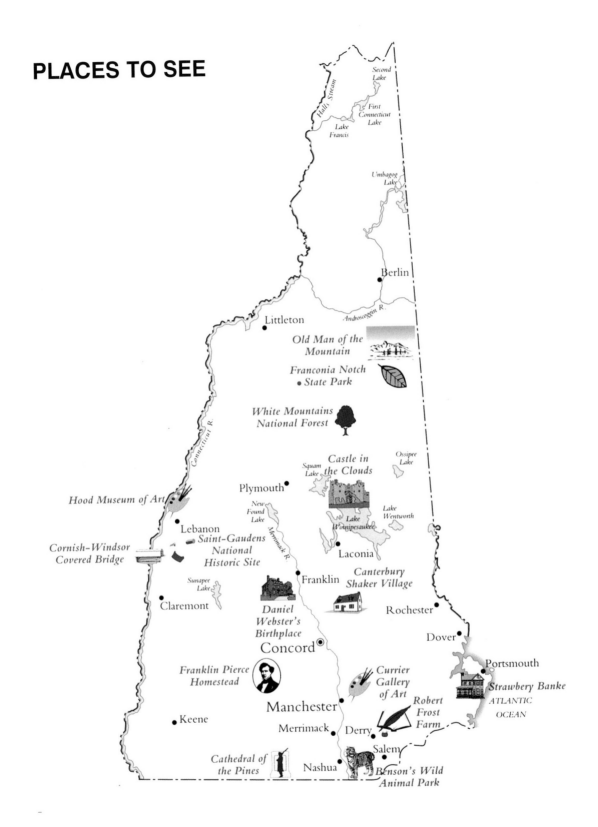

Second Lake

Halls Stream

First Connecticut Lake

Lake Francis

Umbagog Lake

Berlin

Androscoggin R.

Littleton

Old Man of the Mountain

Franconia Notch
State Park

White Mountains
National Forest

Connecticut R.

Castle in the Clouds

Squam Lake

Ossipee Lake

Plymouth

New Found Lake

Lake Wentworth

Hood Museum of Art

Lebanon

Saint-Gaudens
National
Historic Site

Merrimack R.

Lake Winnipesaukee

Laconia

Cornish–Windsor
Covered Bridge

Canterbury
Shaker Village

Franklin

Sunapee Lake

Claremont

Daniel
Webster's
Birthplace

Rochester

Dover

Concord

Portsmouth

Franklin Pierce
Homestead

Currier
Gallery
of Art

Strawbery Banke

ATLANTIC
OCEAN

Manchester

Robert
Frost
Farm

Keene

Merrimack

Derry

Salem

Cathedral of
the Pines

Nashua

Benson's Wild
Animal Park

One of the most popular communities on the shore of Winnipesaukee is Wolfeboro, the oldest summer resort in the United States. It was named after British general James Wolfe, the hero of the Battle of Quebec in the French and Indian Wars. The town is the site of the Libby Museum, founded by a dentist named Henry Libby in 1912. "When I was forty, life began anew for me," Libby wrote. "It was then that I began to see and feel the force and beauty of Nature. . . . I commenced to collect things." Among Libby's collection are Native-American relics and taxidermic animals.

Slightly south of Lake Winnipesaukee, in Franklin, is Daniel Webster's birthplace, a two-room frame house. It contains period antiques and artifacts. To the west of Lake Winnipesaukee, near the Vermont border, is Cornish, where sculptor Augustus Saint-Gaudens created many of his works. Visitors to the Saint-Gaudens National Historic Site can tour his home, which was originally a country tavern, and his studio. About a hundred of his works are on display.

Nearby is the longest covered bridge still in use in the United States. It crosses the Connecticut River from Cornish into Windsor, Vermont. The 460-foot-long bridge was built in 1866. Until the 1940s it cost a dime to cross the bridge; now it is free. There are about fifty covered bridges left in New Hampshire, and they are reminders of simpler times.

The Cornish-Windsor Bridge is the longest two-span wooden covered bridge in the world.

A little southeast of Cornish is Sunapee, which has been a resort community since the mid-1800s.

CASTLE IN THE CLOUDS

In Moultonborough, north of Lake Winnipesaukee, is one of the strangest sights in New Hampshire. High atop a mountain is a stone mansion that appears to be floating in the sky. The legendary Castle in the Clouds is not a medieval mirage but the dream home of a millionaire shoe manufacturer named Thomas Gustave Plant.

In 1911 Plant hired a thousand masons to shape the stone for his fairytale home, which he called Lucknow. Three years and $7 million later, it was finished. The house has sixteen rooms, eight bathrooms, lead doors, and a huge skylight. One secret room, used by Plant for reading, was not entered by another person until after his death in 1941.

Plant's end was not a happy one. He made poor investments and lost all his millions. The house, however, is his legacy, enjoyed by thousands of tourists who visit it each year.

The word *Sunapee* is Algonquian for "flying geese," which is what you might see on a clear day as you take the popular boat cruise across Lake Sunapee.

Farther north near the Vermont border is Hanover, home of Dartmouth College, the ninth-oldest college in the United States and a member of the Ivy League. Dartmouth is famous for its Winter Carnival, begun in 1909 to promote winter sports. The gala event includes displays of ice sculpture, a polar bear swim, and a human dogsled race.

TEN LARGEST CITIES

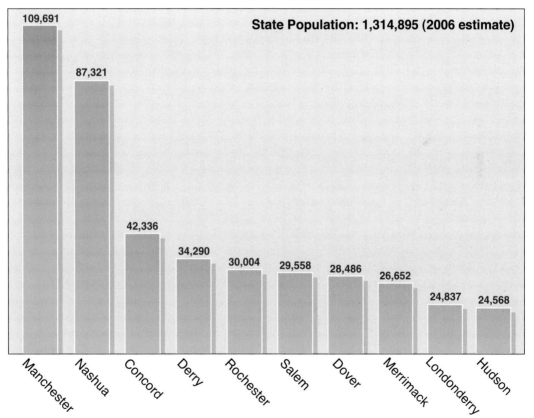

State Population: 1,314,895 (2006 estimate)

City	Population
Manchester	109,691
Nashua	87,321
Concord	42,336
Derry	34,290
Rochester	30,004
Salem	29,558
Dover	28,486
Merrimack	26,652
Londonderry	24,837
Hudson	24,568

NORTHERN NEW HAMPSHIRE

For the adventurous, the north is the place to go in New Hampshire. Here lie the White Mountains with the great Presidential Range, which includes Mount Washington. The White Mountains National Forest covers much of the mountain region and extends into Maine. It has 1,200 miles of hiking trails, 650 miles of fishing streams, and 23 campgrounds. It is the largest wilderness area in New England and the most accessible in the country.

There is more than the mountains themselves to claim a visitor's attention, however. The breaks between the mountains are also worth exploring. Writer Harriet Martineau has called Franconia Notch "the noblest mountain pass in the United States . . . [with] its unusual blend of grandeur and grace." A highlight of Franconia Notch is the Flume, a small but spectacular canyon with a series of pools and waterfalls. Another feature is the Basin, a 20-foot-wide rock pool with sides polished smooth by eons of sand, stone, and running water.

Crawford Notch separates the Presidential Range from the Franconia Mountains and has some of the roughest terrain in the state. Near Pinkham Notch, Tuckerman Ravine is a skier's dream. It is the only place in the United States east of the Rockies where you can enjoy very steep downhill skiing conditions similar to those in the European Alps.

Bethlehem is a popular resort town for relaxation. Part of its popularity comes from its air, which in summer has a reputation for being nearly pollen free. For years the town was a haven for people suffering from hay fever. The American Hay Fever Association was founded in Bethlehem, and its national headquarters were originally located there. People around the world send their Christmas cards to Bethlehem to have them postmarked with the town's famous name.

Water rushes over rocks and through pools at Franconia Notch State Park.

THE OLD MAN OF THE MOUNTAIN

His stern visage, 40 feet from chin to brow, was formed by five ledges of rock. The Old Man of the Mountain adorns everything from state highway signs and the state seal to the New Hampshire Statehood Quarter issued in 2000. Three years after the coin was released, on a May night, this beloved symbol of the Granite State collapsed and was no more. Scientists blame wind and water erosion. Many state residents mourned his loss as they would a close friend and left flowers at the base of Profile Mountain.

The Old Man inspired many writers, most notably Nathaniel Hawthorne, who wrote a story called "The Great Stone Face." Daniel Webster described the Old Man this way:

> Men hang out their signs indicative of their respective trades: Shoemakers hang out a gigantic shoe; jewelers, a monster watch; and the dentist hangs out a gold tooth, but up in the mountains of New Hampshire God Almighty had hung out a sign to show that there he makes men.

On the first anniversary of his "death," a state task force unveiled special viewfinders at the base of the mountain. Looking through one, a viewer sees the Old Man of the Mountain as he looked before that fateful day.

While there are many skiers and tourists in the White Mountains, few residents make their home in this remote region. The largest town in the area is Berlin, with a population of 12,000. It is called the City That Trees Built because its logging industry and paper mills attracted thousands of French Canadians, Russians, and other immigrants decades ago. Among Berlin's most famous residents was Earl Silas Tupper, inventor of the innovative food-storage containers called Tupperware. Berlin is also home to the oldest ski club in America, the Nansen Club, founded in 1872. Nearby is the 262-foot-high Nansen Ski Jump, once the highest steel tower ski jump in the United States.

Even farther north is tiny Pittsburg, population nine hundred, the state's northernmost town and once the center of the Indian Stream Republic. A farming and lumbering community, Pittsburg is the last rest and supply stop for hunters and fishers heading north to the remote Connecticut Lakes. This is about as far north as you can go in New Hampshire before bumping into Canada.

From top to bottom, New Hampshire is full of little treasures. You just have to look around for them in the nooks and crannies.

THE FLAG: The state flag is a blue field containing the state seal surrounded by laurel leaves and nine stars, which indicate that New Hampshire is the ninth state.

THE SEAL: The state seal depicts the frigate Raleigh in the center, a granite boulder on the left, and a rising sun in the background. Around the scene are the words Seal of the State of New Hampshire, the date 1776, and a laurel wreath.

State Survey

Statehood: June 21, 1788

Origin of Name: Named for the English county of Hampshire by Captain John Mason in 1629

Nickname: The Granite State

Capital: Concord

State Motto: Live Free or Die

Bird: Purple finch

Animal: White-tailed deer

Freshwater Fish: Brook trout

Saltwater Fish: Striped bass

Flower: Purple lilac

Wildflower: Pink lady's slipper

Tree: White birch

Insect: Ladybug

Amphibian: Red-spotted newt

Gem: Smoky quartz

Purple finch

Purple lilac

OLD NEW HAMPSHIRE

New Hampshire has the unusual distinction of having nine state songs. "Old New Hampshire" is the official song, and the others are all honorary. Composed in 1926, "Old New Hampshire" was adopted by the legislature in 1949.

Words by Dr. John F. Holmes   **Music by Maurice Hoffman**

Rock: Granite

Mineral: Beryl

Sport: Skiing

GEOGRAPHY

Highest Point: 6,288 feet above sea level, at Mount Washington

Lowest Point: Sea level, along the Atlantic coast

Area: 9,351 square miles

Greatest Distance North to South: 180 miles

Greatest Distance East to West: 93 miles

Bordering States: The Canadian province of Quebec to the north, Massachusetts to the south, Vermont to the west, Maine to the east

Hottest Recorded Temperature: 106 °F at Nashua on July 4, 1911

Coldest Recorded Temperature: −46 °F at Pittsburg on January 28, 1925

Average Annual Precipitation: 42 inches

Major Rivers: Androscoggin, Connecticut, Merrimack, Piscataqua, Saco, Salmon Falls

Major Lakes: Mascoma, Newfound, Ossipee, Squam, Sunapee, Umbagog, Winnipesaukee

Trees: beech, birch, elm, fir, maple, oak, pine, spruce

Wild Plants: Black-eyed Susan, daisy, fireweed, gentian, goldenrod, purple trillium, violet, wild aster

Animals: beaver, black bear, bobcat, chipmunk, coyote, gray squirrel, mink, moose, muskrat, otter, porcupine, raccoon, red fox, red squirrel, skunk, snowshoe hare, white-tailed deer, woodchuck

Birds: blue jay, chickadee, duck, goose, loon, purple finch, robin, sparrow, tern, woodpecker

Fish: bluefish, brook trout, brown trout, bullhead, cask, cod, cunner, flounder, haddock, hake, lake trout, largemouth bass, mackerel, perch, pickerel, pollock, rainbow trout, salmon, smallmouth bass, striped bass, tuna, whitefish

Endangered Animals: arctic tern, Atlantic salmon, bald eagle, dwarfwedge mussel, eastern bluebird, Indiana bat, karner blue butterfly, lynx, osprey, peregrine falcon, pine marten, purple martin, shortnose sturgeon, Sunapee trout, whip-poor-will

Endangered Plants: Robbins' cinquefoil, small whorled pogonia

Porcupine

Eastern bluebird

TIMELINE

New Hampshire History

1600s The region is occupied by the Western Abenaki Indians.

1603 English captain Martin Pring explores the mouth of the Piscataqua River near present-day Portsmouth.

1605 French explorer Samuel de Champlain lands at Piscataqua Bay, sails along the New Hampshire coast, and discovers the Isles of Shoals.

1614 Captain John Smith of England sails along the Atlantic coast and lands on the Isles of Shoals, which he names Smith's Islands.

1622 Sir Ferdinando Gorges and Captain John Mason are granted the land between the Merrimack and Kennebec rivers (present-day New Hampshire and Maine).

1623 David Thomson founds the first settlement at Ordiorne's Point in Little Harbor, now called Rye; Edward Hilton settles Hilton's Point, now Dover.

1629 John Mason names the area between the Merrimack and Piscataqua rivers New Hampshire.

1638–1639 Clergyman John Wheelwright founds Exeter; colonists led by the Reverend Stephen Bachiler found Hampton.

1641 The four New Hampshire towns place themselves under the government of Massachusetts.

1679 New Hampshire separates from Massachusetts and becomes a royal province.

1692 New Hampshire becomes a separate province.

1734 A religious revival known as the Great Awakening sweeps through New Hampshire.

1756 New Hampshire's first newspaper, the *New Hampshire Gazette*, is established in Portsmouth.

1770 Dartmouth College opens in Hanover.

1774 Paul Revere rides to New Hampshire to warn of British military buildup in Massachusetts; some four hundred colonists capture military supplies from the British at Fort William and Mary in New Castle and provide arms for the Battle of Bunker Hill.

1775 The First Provincial Congress meets at Exeter; the Revolutionary War breaks out in Massachusetts, and hundreds of New Hampshirites join the fight.

1776 New Hampshire becomes the first colony to declare independence, six months before signing the Declaration of Independence.

1777 Vermont separates from New Hampshire and creates an independent republic.

1784 The New Hampshire state constitution is adopted.

1788 New Hampshire is the ninth state to ratify the United States Constitution.

1808 Concord becomes the state capital.

1819 The State House is completed; a religious toleration act prohibits taxation for church purposes.

1833 The nation's first free, tax-supported public library is founded at Peterborough.

1852 New Hampshire native Franklin Pierce is elected fourteenth president of the United States.

1916 The New Hampshire presidential primary is held for the first time; four years later it becomes the nation's first primary.

1917–1918 Portsmouth Naval Shipyard becomes an important builder of warships during World War I.

1923 The University of New Hampshire is founded.

1961 New Hampshirite Alan Shepard is the first American astronaut to travel in space.

1963 New Hampshire legalizes a state lottery, the nation's first since 1894.

1986 Concord high school teacher Christa McAuliffe and six others perish when the space shuttle *Challenger* explodes seconds after liftoff.

1988 New Hampshire joins eight other states in a suit to force the Environmental Protection Agency to establish acid rain controls in the Midwest.

1990 New Hampshirite David Souter is appointed associate justice of the U.S. Supreme Court.

1997 Democrat Jeanne Shaheen is elected New Hampshire's first woman governor.

2006 Democrat Carol Shea-Porter is elected New Hampshire's first U.S. congresswoman.

ECONOMY

Agricultural Products: apples, beef cattle, berries, Christmas trees, eggs, sweet corn, hay, maple syrup, milk, poultry

Manufactured Products: computers, electric lamps, electronics equipment, lumber, metals, paper products, plastics, wood products

Natural Resources: clay, feldspar, forests, granite, gravel, sand

Business and Trade: banking, education, finance, health care, insurance, real estate, tourism

Lumber

CALENDAR OF CELEBRATIONS

Dartmouth Winter Carnival In Hanover every February, elaborate ice sculptures grace the Dartmouth Green. This celebration of winter also includes ski jumping.

Mount Washington Valley Chocolate Festival Earn your chocolate by cross-country skiing from inn to inn and picking up sweets at each stop. This delicious festival takes place in North Conway in February.

World Championship Sled Dog Derby For three days in Laconia in February onlookers can watch colorful teams of sled dogs race.

Frostbite Follies Sleigh rides, ski races, ski movies, and broom hockey are all included in these follies, which are held in Franconia in February.

Maple Season Tours In Bethlehem during April, visitors can attend workshops to learn about gathering sap and boiling it down to make maple syrup.

New Hampshire Annual Sheep and Wool Festival This May festival in New Boston includes border collie demonstrations. Shearing, carding, and spinning are also demonstrated.

Quacktillion and Wildquack River Festival In Jackson Village in May, fans can cheer on one of two thousand rubber ducks as they race down the river; they can even be rented for five dollars.

Dartmouth Winter Carnival

Market Square Days Celebration This lively street fair takes place in Portsmouth in June. It includes music, booths selling food and crafts, and a clambake.

International Children's Festival This June festival in Somersworth has four entertainment stages, including one just for kids, a craft fair, food booths, and a hands-on crafts tent for children.

Revolutionary War Days Each July Exeter celebrates the Revolutionary War with battle reenactments, period crafts and antiques, and a visit from George Washington at the American Independence Museum.

League of New Hampshire Craftsmen's Fair Mount Sunapee State Park in Sunapee is the site of the nation's oldest crafts fair. The nine-day August gathering includes music, art exhibits, and crafts demonstrations.

Lancaster Fair Every Labor Day weekend, Lancaster hosts this old-fashioned country fair. There are thrill rides, a 4-H animal competition, displays of vegetables and handicrafts, oxen and horse pulling, and harness racing.

Hampton Beach Seafood Festival This celebrated event was begun in 1988 and is held on the weekend after Labor Day. More than 200,000 people descend on Hampton Beach each year to enjoy the many delicacies offered.

Riverfest Celebration For three days every September Manchester sparkles with fireworks, entertainment, and canoe competitions.

Lancaster Fair

World Mud Bowl Each September in North Conway, this annual charity football game is played in knee-deep mud.

Harvest Day This Shaker-style celebration of the harvest in Canterbury each October includes exhibits and games.

Oh! Christmas Tree In Bethlehem each December, you can enjoy wreath and ornament making, and a hay-wagon tour of a Christmas tree plantation. You can even pick your own tree to cut.

Candlelight Stroll at Strawbery Banke Join carolers for a Christmas stroll in Portsmouth through nine historic homes decorated for the holiday season. More than a thousand candles light Strawbery Banke's 10-acre grounds.

First Night New Hampshire There are First Night celebrations in Concord, Keene, Portsmouth, and Wolfeboro. This final night of the year typically starts with a parade and ends with fireworks.

STATE STARS

Josiah Bartlett (1720–1795) was a Revolutionary War patriot and New Hampshire delegate to the Second Continental Congress. Bartlett was the second person to sign the Declaration of Independence. He was also chief justice of the U.S. Supreme Court, the first governor of New Hampshire, and a practicing physician for forty-five years.

Amy Marcy Beach (1867–1944), the most prominent American woman composer of her time, was born in Henniker. In 1896 she composed the *Gaelic Symphony*, the first published symphonic work by an American woman. In 1923 she cofounded the Association of American Women Composers.

Amy Marcy Beach

Elizabeth Gardner Bouguereau (1837–1922) was an artist born in Exeter. She was the first woman to exhibit a painting at the Paris Salon of the French Academy of Art and the first woman awarded a Gold Medal by the exclusive academy.

Alice Brown (1856–1948) wrote short stories and plays describing the people and places of New Hampshire, including *Meadow-Grass: Tales of New England* and *Children of Earth*. She was born in Hampton Falls.

Ken Burns (1953–   ) is a famous documentary filmmaker who was born in New York City. After receiving a degree in film studies in 1975, Burns formed his own company, Florentine Films. His documentaries include *Baseball*, *Lewis and Clark*, and the eleven-hour Emmy-winning *Civil War*. He resides in Walpole.

Benjamin Champney (1817–1907), who was born in New Ipswich, was an artist and one of the founders of the Boston Art Club. After painting landscapes in Europe in the 1840s, he began landscape painting in the White Mountains of New Hampshire. He founded an art colony in the North Conway Area.

Charles Anderson Dana (1819–1897) was a journalist who served as U.S. assistant secretary of war under President Abraham Lincoln. From 1868 to 1897 he was the owner and editor of the *New York Sun*, an influential newspaper. He was born in Hinsdale.

Tomie dePaola (1934–) is one of the most popular children's book illustrators and writers in the United States. He won a Caldecott Honor Award in 1976 for his illustrations in *Strega Nona*. He lives in New London.

Mary Baker Eddy (1821–1910) was born in Bow, near Concord. During her recovery from a severe fall in 1866, she turned to the Bible and formulated a spiritual and metaphysical system of healing that became known as Christian Science. In 1908 she founded the *Christian Science Monitor*, an acclaimed newspaper that has maintained a wide circulation.

Mike Flanagan (1951–) pitched for the Baltimore Orioles and the Toronto Blue Jays. In 1979 Flanagan won the Cy Young Award for winning more baseball games than any other pitcher in the American League. He was born in Manchester.

Elizabeth Gurley Flynn (1890–1964), who was born in Concord, was the first woman to head the Communist Party in the United States. President of the American Communist Party from 1961 to 1964, she helped factory workers throughout the United States gain more rights and improve working conditions. In 1920 Flynn helped found the American Civil Liberties Union, an organization that promotes citizens' rights.

Robert Frost (1874–1963) was a four-time Pulitzer Prize-winning poet who wrote about rural New England. One volume of his poetry is called *New Hampshire*. Frost attended Dartmouth College in Hanover and later lived on farms in Derry and Franconia.

John Irving (1941–   ) is a novelist known for creating eccentric characters. One of his best-known books, *The World According to Garp*, was nominated for the National Book Award and was made into a movie. Another of Irving's books, *The Hotel New Hampshire*, also was made into a movie. Irving was born in Exeter.

John Irving

Kancamagus (1644?–1691?) was the last chief of the Pennacook Indians in New Hampshire. When war broke out between the British and the Indians, Kancamagus led his people to Canada to escape attacks. A New Hampshire highway following that route is named after him.

Christa McAuliffe (1948–1986), a Concord social studies teacher, was chosen by NASA in 1985 to be the first private citizen in space. She was killed when the space shuttle *Challenger* exploded over the Atlantic Ocean 73 seconds after liftoff on January 28, 1986.

Christa McAuliffe

Bob Montana (1920–1975) created the popular comic strip *Archie*, which described the lives of American teenagers, in 1942. Many of the characters were based on classmates from Montana's high school in Manchester.

Franklin Pierce (1804–1869) was the fourteenth president of the United States. The only American chief executive from New Hampshire, he was born in Hillsboro. A dark-horse candidate, Pierce won the Democratic presidential nomination on the forty-ninth ballot. He became the youngest president, at age forty-eight, up to that time. Pierce presided over the opening of Japan to international trade and extended the United States at its southwestern border by overseeing the Gadsden Purchase. His proslavery policies earned him the hatred of many Northerners, however, and he did not win renomination in 1856.

Charles Alfred Pillsbury (1842–1899) was a flour miller born in Warner. In Minnesota he established a flour mill that became C.A. Pillsbury and Company, one of the world's largest flour producers in the 1880s.

Eleanor H. Porter (1868–1920) was a children's author born in Littleton. She wrote *Pollyanna*, a book about a perpetually cheerful little girl, which sold more than a million copies and has been made into several films.

J. D. Salinger (1919–) is the author of *Catcher in the Rye*, a classic novel about the problems a teenage boy faces growing up, as well as many short stories. He lives near Cornish.

J. D. Salinger

Alan Shepard (1924–1998) was born in East Derry. After serving in World War II, Shepard became a navy test pilot and joined the astronaut program. The first American in space, he orbited Earth in the rocket *Freedom 7* in May 1961. Years later he commanded the third mission to the moon in *Apollo 14* and became the fifth man to walk on the Moon.

Earl Silas Tupper (1907–1983) founded Tupperware. He began selling his plastic storage containers to stores in the mid-1940s, but they did not become popular until a decade later when housewives organized home parties to sell them. Tupper was born in Berlin.

Daniel Webster (1782–1852), who was born in Salisbury (now Franklin), was a lawyer, orator, and statesman. He was a U.S. congressman, a U.S. senator, and U.S. secretary of state. He is best remembered for his speeches, especially his inspiring words recalled by the Union soldiers during the Civil War: "Liberty and Union, now and forever, one and inseparable!"

Eleazar Wheelock (1711–1779) was an American educator and Congregationalist minister. He was the founder and first president of Dartmouth College in Hanover.

George Hoyt Whipple (1878–1976) was a pathologist who discovered how to reverse the dangerous effects of a blood disease called anemia. For this work he won the 1934 Nobel Prize in Physiology or Medicine. He was born in Ashland.

Annalee's Doll Museum (Meredith) This museum is home to more than a thousand flexible felt dolls, three hundred of which are on display at any one time. The dolls, created by Annalee Thorndike, are set against a backdrop of dioramas depicting New Hampshire scenes.

Canterbury Shaker Village (Canterbury) This village was founded in 1792 by the Shaker religious sect. Buildings, furniture, and crafts are on display, demonstrating Shaker craftsmanship and design.

Castle in the Clouds (Moultonborough) Visit the castle overlooking Lake Winnipesaukee built by millionaire Thomas Gustave Plant in 1913. The 5,200-acre estate includes waterfalls, ponds, streams, trails, and great views of the countryside. The castle was built without nails and has doors made of lead.

Cathedral of the Pines (Rindge) This outdoor cathedral is used for nondenominational services. The Women's Memorial Bell Tower, built of local stone, honors American women killed in wars, and the Altar of the Nation recognizes all American war casualties. Congress made this shrine a national memorial in 1957.

The Christa McAuliffe Planetarium (Concord) This planetarium, a memorial to the first civilian in space, has the most advanced planetarium projection system in the world. It can simulate space travel up to 600 light-years from Earth and one million years into the future or the past. Look through the 40-foot dome telescope, or check out the tornado tubes, magnetic marbles, and other hands-on exhibits.

Conway Scenic Railroad

(North Conway) Ride in the big red coach pulled by an old-fashioned steam locomotive or by a diesel electric engine from a 1874 Victorian railroad station preserved as a museum. Railroad artifacts, lanterns, and old timetables and tickets are on display.

Daniel Webster's Birthplace

(Franklin) This small cabin houses replicas of period furnishings along with childhood mementos of Daniel Webster, the legendary lawyer, orator, and statesman.

Franconia Notch State Park

(Easton) The famous Old Man of the Mountain rock formation, which looked like the side of an old man's face, once stood above Profile Lake; it collapsed in 2003. The park also features Flume Gorge, an 800-foot chasm with a waterfall, and an eighty-passenger aerial tramway at Cannon Mountain that offers great views of the scenery.

Conway Scenic Railroad

Franconia Notch State Park

Franklin Pierce Homestead (Hillsboro) See the restored 1804 childhood home of the fourteenth president of the United States. It was designated a national historic landmark in 1961.

Heritage New Hampshire (Glen) Experience a three-hundred-year review of New Hampshire history. Photographs, dioramas, rides, animation, and period characters all help to bring the history of New Hampshire to life. Hear a speech by George Washington or climb aboard a ship traveling from a seventeenth-century village in England to the New World.

John Paul Jones House (Portsmouth) This was the temporary home of the Revolutionary War hero who made the famous exclamation "I have not yet begun to fight!" Costumes, glassware, guns, portraits, and documents of the late eighteenth century are on display.

Lake Winnipesaukee (Laconia) The 70 square miles of Lake Winnipesaukee, New Hampshire's largest lake, provide plenty of opportunity for sightseeing, boating, fishing, and water sports. On the east side of the lake, at the Wolfeboro Historical Society Museum, are an eighteenth-century home, a nineteenth-century firehouse, and an 1820 school.

Monadnock State Park (Jaffrey) This park is the home of Mount Monadnock, the most-climbed mountain in North America. Six New England states can be seen from the top; sometimes even the Boston skyline can be made out.

Mount Washington State Park (Crawford Notch) This park includes the Mount Washington Cog Railway, which opened in 1869 and is like a slow roller-coaster ride and moving museum. The track grade to the summit is the second steepest in the world and was the first of its type.

Museum of New Hampshire History (Concord) This museum features exhibits depicting New Hampshire's history, from the Abenaki Indians to the settlers of Portsmouth. There are also a replica of a fire tower with a view of the city and an original Concord Coach, a nineteenth-century stagecoach.

New England Ski Museum (Franconia) Here you can see a history of skiing in the East, with a collection of ski photos, old trophies, skis and bindings, boots, and ski apparel from the late 1800s.

Old Fort No. 4 (Charlestown) Visit a reconstruction of a stockaded village as it looked during the French and Indian Wars. During the summer, the staff wears costumes, demonstrates eighteenth-century crafts, and reenacts battles.

Ruggles Mine (Grafton) See the mine where production of mica in the United States began in 1803. An estimated 150 different minerals and gemstones can be found there. Collect some and take them home.

Saint-Gaudens National Historic Site (Cornish) This is the former summer home and studio of the famous sculptor Augustus Saint-Gaudens. The estate includes a barn/studio, an art gallery, and formal gardens. The sculptor's works, as well as sketches and casting molds, are scattered throughout.

Saint-Gaudens National Historic Site

Santa's Village (Jefferson) Feed reindeer, browse through the shops, and have a snack at the village eateries. There are rides and live shows daily.

Science Center of New Hampshire (Squam Lake) This 20-acre science center offers woodland and lake excursions, live animal programs, bird-watching, stargazing, and other informative and fun programs. Squam Lake is where the movie *On Golden Pond* was filmed.

Story Land (Glen) Meet Humpty Dumpty and the Three Pigs at this theme park. You can also venture on an African safari, ride on a swan boat, and cool off in the park's "sprayground."

Strawbery Banke (Portsmouth) Strawbery Banke, named for the wild strawberries that once grew there, portrays the evolving life of a waterfront neighborhood from the 1690s to the 1950s. The site includes 42 historic buildings on 10 acres.

FUN FACTS

The first potato in the United States was planted at Londonderry Common Field (now Derry) in 1719.

On April 12, 1934, workers at Mount Washington's weather observatory witnessed the most powerful gust of wind ever recorded on land other than during a tornado. The wind speed was measured at 231 miles per hour.

More people have climbed Mount Monadnock than any other mountain in North America. In the entire world only Mount Fuji in Japan has been climbed more times.

The Brattle organ in Saint John's Church in Portsmouth, named after its first owner, Thomas Brattle, is said to be the oldest pipe organ in the United States. It dates back to 1708 and is still played on special occasions.

More than half the remaining covered bridges in New England are in New Hampshire, including the longest one in the country—the 460-foot Cornish-Windsor Bridge, which crosses the Connecticut River.

Tiny Dixville Notch is the first community to vote in presidential primary elections. Voting starts just after midnight on Primary Day.

Find Out More

Want to know more about New Hampshire? Check the library or bookstore for these titles:

GENERAL STATE BOOKS

Heinrichs, Ann. *Welcome to the U.S.A.: New Hampshire.* Chanhassen, MN: The Child's World, 2005.

Smolan, Rick, and David Elliot Cohen. *New Hampshire 24/7.* London: DK Adult, 2004.

Smolik, Jane Petrlik. *The Great New Hampshire Puzzle Book.* Wenham, MA: MidRun Press, 2007.

SPECIAL INTEREST BOOKS

Clayton, John. *You Know You're in New Hampshire When . . . : 101 Quintessential Places, People, Events, Customs, Lingo, and Eats of the Granite State.* Guilford, CT: Globe Pequot, 2005.

Mis, Melody S. *The Colony of New Hampshire: A Primary Source History.* New York: PowerKids Press, 2006.

Streissguth, Thomas. *Christa McAuliff.* Mankato, MN: Bridgestone Books, 2003.

Venezia, Mike. *Franklin Pierce: Fourteenth President 1853–1857.* Danbury, CT: Children's Press, 2006.

VIDEOS

New Hampshire's Mountains and Lakes. 30 mins., Site Productions.

New Hampshire Steam Railroads. Total Marketing Services.

WEB SITES

New Hampshire: You're Going To Love It Here
http://www.visitnh.gov
This is the official site of the New Hampshire Division of Travel and Tourism Development. It offers listings of things to do, events, and a trip planner.

New Hampshire: Where New Hampshire Clicks
http://www.nh.com
This comprehensive site includes the latest news from New Hampshire, a photo gallery, and much more.

Index

Page numbers in **boldface** are illustrations and charts.

ABOUT THE AUTHOR

Steven Otfinoski is the author of *Georgia* in the Celebrate the States series and *Maryland* and *Washington* in the It's My State! series for Marshall Cavendish Benchmark. He has also written more than twenty other non-fiction titles for Marshall Cavendish. Otfinoski lives in Connecticut with his wife, Beverly, an editor and high school English teacher.